How to Grow a Backbone

How to Grow a Backbone

10 Strategies
for Gaining Power and
Influence at Work

SUSAN MARSHALL

CB
CONTEMPORARY BOOKS

Library of Congress Cataloging-in-Publication Data

Marshall, Susan A.
    How to Grow a Backbone : 10 strategies for gaining power and influence at
work / Susan A. Marshall.
        p.   cm.
    Includes bibliographical references and index.
    ISBN 0-8092-2494-1
    1. Success.   2. Success in business.   3. Assertiveness (Psychology)
4. Interpersonal communication.   I. Title.
HF5386.M36   2000
650.1—dc21   00-29474
                                                                        CIP

Cover and interior design by Jennifer Locke
Cover and interior illustrations by Art Glazer
Author photo by Susan Benton

Published by Contemporary Books
A division of NTC/Contemporary Publishing Group, Inc.
4255 West Touhy Avenue, Lincolnwood (Chicago), Illinois 60712-1975 U.S.A.
Copyright © 2000 by Susan Marshall
Printed in the United States of America
International Standard Book Number: 0-8092-2494-1
00 01 02 03 04 05 MV 19 18 17 16 15 14 13 12 11 10 9 8 7 6 5 4 3 2 1

To my sister, Lori, who without realizing it demonstrates backbone in a way that has influenced my thinking for years.

Contents

Foreword

THIS BOOK IS a gift to every one who works in today's pressure-filled society and wants to make more of a difference in the world. It's a gift to bring home to your loved ones as well.

I believe that each of us is born with a unique potential that defines a destiny, not only at work but also in life. Few of us ever glimpse this hidden, one-of-a-kind potential, much less liberate and explore it. Instead, even when we sense opportunity calling, all too often we find ourselves repeating old habits, saying nothing, getting by, going along, or giving in. One of the key reasons is a lack of backbone.

In this compelling and memorable book, Susan Marshall challenges each reader to step forward in life and at work. She encourages you to consider specific, practical ways to increase your genuine individual power and influence.

In my research, I have found that when people successfully face challenges and do the best work of their lives, it's largely because they have found a way to generate uncommon levels of energy, passion, inner-strength, and commitment. *How to Grow a Backbone* is a valuable contribution to the literature and offers vital reading for leaders and professionals at every level of organizations.

—Robert K. Cooper, Ph.D., chair of Advance Excellence Systems, and bestselling author of *The Performance Edge* and *Executive EQ: Emotional Intelligence in Leadership & Organizations*

Preface

WELCOME TO THE world of business, where chaos reigns and organizations desperately need their people to be at the top of their game.

Welcome to the world where downsizings, rightsizings, reengineering, and assorted other management remedies have driven people to the edge of cynicism and, worse, into protective cubbyholes.

You'd love to have every ounce of your intelligence tapped and channeled for the good of your organization and your career, wouldn't you? To make decisions, take action, and feel proud of your contributions.

Bet you'd be energized to say what you think without fearing reprisal. To be respectful and straightforward in all your dealings. To devote your attention to matters that you know are important instead of being led around on a leash crafted of intimidation and fear. Wouldn't it be refreshing to feel a little more in control of your life at work?

You can do all of these things, provided you have a strong and healthy backbone.

A lot of workers complain today about not having the chance to prove themselves. They say bureaucracy shuts them down, or a traditional hierarchy with its established pecking order keeps them stuck in places where their talents and skills are wasted. Some complain about bias, discrimination, favoritism, and even corruption in their companies. But when many of these folks get into situations that test what they're made of, the oddest thing happens: They play it safe. They clam up, hedge their posi-

> **Business, we know, is now so complex and difficult, the survival of firms so hazardous in an environment increasingly unpredictable, competitive, and fraught with danger, that their existence depends on the day-to-day mobilization of every ounce of intelligence.**
>
> KONOSUKE MATSUSHITA, CEO,
> MATSUSHITA ELECTRIC INDUSTRIAL COMPANY

tions, and take pains to be politically correct. They give all kinds of excuses for why things can't be the way they would like them to be, and they're short on the backbone needed to initiate change.

This may be understandable, given the chaotic nature of organizational change over the past decade, but understanding the reasons why you're tentative doesn't change the need for you to grow out of this hesitancy. Business is tough, and it's only going to get tougher.

Top thinkers in the field frequently use analogies to help people understand the nature and demands of the business environment. *Jamming*, John Kao's bestseller, describes how jazz musicians gather for jam sessions, creating exciting new music on the fly. He stresses that these freewheeling and wildly improvisational sessions are based on sound fundamentals and learned trust. "Jazz musicians must work within a structure. They agree on who is to play when, and on a loose conception of key or total center, and they let a stable beat determine a solo's rhythmic shape." Musicians understand and follow rules of grammar and timing even as they're creating all-new sounds together.

Jazz musician Gary Burton, three-time Grammy Award winner, member of the Percussion Hall of Fame, and executive vice president of Berklee College of Music in Boston, tells international audiences the same thing: "Music—even jazz—has structure. Without structure, there is no way for others to understand what you're trying to communicate. When you know the basics well, you can improvise, building new, more interesting, and more exciting creations."

Structure . . . bureaucracy. Which is it? Shades of the same thing?

People with backbone see necessary structure. People without backbone see bureaucracy and fear it.

Many of us were taught to respect (and be a little afraid of) authority, to be patient learners, to defer to those who know more than we do or who, by virtue of time spent in a position, have greater stature. These lessons were good; they helped us to live and work together because they defined a structure and a guide for workplace behaviors. Let's say these are the fundamentals upon which we improvise, the basics from which we draw to "jam."

The problem today (and it's growing rapidly) is that so much of what we were taught about the business environment is obviously not true anymore. Longevity does not mean enhanced knowledge, nor does it mean job security. Older people are not necessarily smarter anymore. Traditional standard business practices don't apply as they used to.

The basics seem outdated. Old structures that used to support progress now seem to have become barriers to progress. Rules of grammar and timing are no longer known with clarity because we have imported many new languages into our organizations and ways of being. The old is burdensome, and we try to innovate our way to the future. But, just as with jazz music, the fundamentals must be understood first. What are they?

You have a stake in the answer. You can't wait for someone else to decide. You can't sit patiently until good things develop. You can't trust someone else (a friend of the family) or something else (an equal-opportunity mandate) to get you where you want to go. Businesses need people who are willing to invest their minds, their talents, and their energies in helping the enterprises grow and succeed. Businesses need people who can think clearly, speak plainly, work collaboratively in a mature and productive way, and make a real contribution to the future. Businesses need people who are willing to take a calculated risk with eyes wide open and contingency plans prepared. In short, businesses need people with backbone.

That's why, if you want to be a player in business, you need to grow yours.

This book was written to challenge you. To make you think. To open your eyes to what's going on around you. To teach you how to be a lot smarter than you are now. To encourage you to listen more carefully, watch more keenly, and find ways that others may overlook to take command of situations, events, and your future. It's meant to help you make your own decisions and then act on them.

If you'll invest the time to grow a backbone—a solid, trustworthy sense of strength and conviction—you'll enjoy greater power and influence in your career. Guaranteed. You'll also enjoy a greater sense of perspective, peace, and stability. It's going to take work. It's going to take time. But I promise you that it'll be an interesting and entertaining journey.

Acknowledgments

I DON'T KNOW when I first realized that for unfathomable reasons, strong people captured and held my attention. I know I was little. And I know that whenever it first occurred to me, I became immediately fascinated with how strong people got that way and why I was so taken with them. Over time, I realized that I wanted to be like them.

With this book, I hope to share some of what I've learned with the many people who wish they could be stronger, more confident, and bolder in how they make choices about their professional lives. It contains stories of many real people, though no real names have been used. It's funny: we don't like to know people are watching us, but we do like to know that someone has learned something from us. My sincere thanks to all the subjects in this book. I've learned from them all.

In addition, several people stand out as having more than passing influence on my Backbone journey. To remember and acknowledge all of them would constitute material for a bad awards night speech. I'll spare you that. But there are several who stand out.

Mr. Jacobson, high school journalism teacher, taught me to stop and think before allowing words to tumble helter-skelter from my mouth. As I hemmed and hawed my way through an answer one day in class, he whipped a piece of chalk at me and roared, "Keep your mouth shut until you know what you want to say!" I was stunned into silence and a second later I grinned with appreciation. These days such an act would probably be considered child abuse. In retrospect, I found it to be child shaping. We need more of it.

As I thought ahead to college, I was full of big ideas and grand dreams of academic success. With the arrogance of youth, I expected my parents to recognize my brilliance and open the family coffers in support of its nurturing. But I was one of six kids growing up in a society that still favored sending boys to college and showing indifference to the academic aspirations of girls, which it considered fickle. There were three younger brothers at home and precious little money to fund advanced education. Still, I was shocked and disappointed when my parents said, "You're smart enough. If you want to go, you'll find a way."

Well it took a long time and a lot of struggle, but eventually I did find a way. What I learned in the process has been invaluable. I didn't like a lot of what I went through. I wouldn't repeat it. But I'm glad to have had the experience. It made me stronger, less afraid of trying things, and less sensitive to failure. I learned to color outside life's boxes, and that has made an incredible difference in my life. So Mom and Dad, though there was discomfort, embarrassment, and real anguish surrounding those early days, I thank you for making me pave my own way.

At work, people like Andy Weber helped me continue on the path of growth. A coworker and special friend, Andy once called me "the Mike Tyson" of my work group. This embarrassed me a bit, but I was privately flattered to know that people relied on me to take the lead when controversial issues arose.

My friend Charlie Krause, a management consultant for many years, suggested to me some time ago that I ought to give serious consideration to writing a book. I laughed it off but felt the stirrings of a childhood dream to do that very thing. Thanks, Charlie, for waking the sleeping aspiration.

Peter C. Marshall has probably the greatest investment in this book. He fed and housed me, listened with glazed over eyes to endless variations of my stories, and reminded me of my dream and ability in all the moments when I doubted. This book would not exist without his support, encouragement, and sponsorship.

Finally, the wonderful folks at NTC/Contemporary Publishing worked their magic to make this dream a reality. Matthew Carnicelli was enthusiastic about the book's concept from the get-go. The talented illustrator (Art Glazer) has lent a delightful personality to my words through his imaginative drawings. Nancy Hall has been impressive in her follow-through and competence at every stage of production.

There are many others who could be mentioned here. As we reflect on our lives, stories surface at different times and for different reasons. To everyone who has shown me the importance—and the joy—of a healthy backbone, I offer this work in gratitude.

And to my daughters, Jenny and Kelly, who gave me unconditional love throughout this project and saucy challenge in the moments when I needed it most, I thank you for your special guidance as we've grown together. You have touched me and shaped me in ways I will never forget.

How to Grow a Backbone

Introduction
Backbone Basics

LET'S SEE. Organizations have reengineered themselves. Downsized. Rightsized. Merged, morphed, and delved deeply into the concept of virtuality. Workers, as a result, have learned that they are (pick one) inadequate, outdated, unnecessary overhead, too old, too young, too something else. This is not a happy thing for workers, and, to the extent that they buy it, it's not a good thing for business in general.

The world will continue to change. Competition will continue to plague us if that's how we want to view it, and business will always need to reconsider past practices in light of today's realities. This means that instead of continuing to pick the scabs of healed-over wounds caused by mean and uncaring companies, workers need to figure out what they're good at, find the best place to do what they're good at, and enjoy the benefits of contributing to something bigger and more exciting than themselves.

> **In the organization of the future, employees must become more autonomous, self-directed, and self-motivated.**
> DAVE ULRICH, CO-AUTHOR,
> *THE BOUNDARYLESS ORGANIZATION: BREAKING THE CHAINS OF ORGANIZATIONAL STRUCTURE*

Damning organizations for their callousness in relations with workers has been in vogue for some time. Certainly the myriad attempts to find the ideal combination of competitiveness, sleekness, and just-right profitability have raised questions and eyebrows right along with frustration levels for years. Figuring out the best organizational structure to compete now and in the future is no easy task, and floundering, to a certain extent, should be expected.

1

But before you begin to think I'm defending organizational ineptitude, let me pose a question: Who are the people behind these organizations? The ubiquitous "they"—those organizational meanies—are people who came from somewhere, learned some things, earned spots of decision-making authority, and now call the shots as they see them in the midst of chaotic change.

I'll ask another question: If these people are so nasty, if their decisions are so wrong, and if history continues to show how ill-fated their ideas are, why do others continue to heed them? Are we confused?

Since Tom Peters and Bob Waterman launched the new era of corporate excellence back in 1982, business literature has run the gamut from principled leadership and the learning organization to optimal organizational structures, total quality management (TQM), quantum physics, chaos theory, intellectual capital, and emotional intelligence. These and many other solid, sensible concepts have alternatively stimulated the thinking and imagination of workers and caused them to be disheartened by how quickly such ideas come and go in the workplace.

Many people in today's organizations are suffering from the fatigue that accompanies these seesaw emotions. They feel hopeful about the prospects for positive change when they welcome new leaders, reconfigure organizational groupings that have proved ineffective, or initiate new policies designed to give more workers greater freedom and autonomy to get the job done.

Yet, in many cases—too many—we eventually see a diminishment of hope and effort as the promising new precept slides into the soon-passed fad of the month.

In their insightful book, *The Witch Doctors: Making Sense of the Management Gurus*, authors John Micklethwait and Adrian Wooldridge note that "there is nothing necessarily wrong with trying out ideas." But "for every theory dragging companies one way, there are two other theories dragging it in another." The authors ask whether management gurus want total defect-free quality or speed. Distinctive, clearly defined culture or diversity? A unifying vision or practical acceptance of the ambiguity of the times? Barring clear answers to these and other pressing concerns, they conclude, "usually, they [gurus] end up telling managers to do both."

No wonder so many smart people seem to be running to and fro, thinking first this, then being persuaded to think that. What's a person to do? Well, you can continue to turn to various experts for the solution du jour, or you can take another tack. You can slow down. Sort things out. Understand what you're trying to accomplish. Acknowledge reality. And then decide for yourself.

To paraphrase Mr. Ulrich, whose quote opens this Introduction: In the organization of the future, employees must develop and demonstrate healthy backbones.

What Is Backbone?

Backbone can be defined as "firm and resolute character." *Gumption*, a close cousin to backbone, comprises common sense, enterprise, and initiative. Backbone at work might look like courage. Perhaps there is someone you will always remember for having the *cajones* to stand up for something that was important but a little risky. Or someone who held the line on an unpopular decision. Or the person who stuck to his guns in the face of ridicule or threat. Or the person who refused to be drawn into an ugly argument and simply held her tongue.

Maybe *character* is a word you associate with backbone. Or *integrity*. Or *boldness*.

Backbone has been used throughout the years to suggest all these things. More recently, backbone has become digitized, technologized—it's the main structural or anchoring base of a network. (Another great ancient idea updated for the Information Age.) I recently heard a wine-grower comment that a certain grape gave backbone to one of his wines. The uses of the word are many, but they all suggest that backbone is an essential element of an organism that gives strength and support to other elements or systems.

The type of backbone we'll address throughout this book—the kind that will bring you greater power and influence at work—is composed of three major segments: competence, confidence, and risk taking.

Backbone Anatomy

Competence

Competence is the state of having means sufficient for the necessities of life. Being competent means having requisite ability or qualities—being fit. It also means rightfully belonging and being legally qualified or capable. In short, having competence means you have the wherewithal to do what you're expected to do in the environment within which you dwell.

Think about that. Your success starts with your level of competence, not with whom you know (although this always helps) or where you come from, but what you're able to do.

Competence encompasses a wide spectrum of mastery and maestroism. It covers every known human activity, from cooking to writing computer code, from designing nuclear submarines to discerning baby talk. Our respect for this fantastic array of competence is evident in the slew of awards we grant to duly note masterworks.

Take patents, for example. The 1989 *New York Public Library Desk Reference* stated that the Patent and Trademark Office (PTO) "currently receives about 100,000 applications for patents each year, and it has granted more than 4.5 million since 1790." That was in 1989. Patent attorney Dinesh Agarwal later observed that the 5 millionth patent was issued on March 19, 1991. That's a half million more patents in less than two years. In 1993, the PTO received approximately 189,000 applications for patents. That's an 89 percent increase in four years. And in 1995, the PTO was *issuing* patents at the rate of 113,000 per year—13 percent more than the number of *applications* it received just six years earlier. That's quite a tribute to competence.

But recall the phrase used in the definition of competence: "requisite ability." *Requisite* means "necessary, essential." This distinction stipulates that abilities, qualities, and capabilities are directed toward something. Survival, leadership, teamwork, creativity, innovation, you name it: In business, the need for competence is enormous. And in a world that has erupted with new ideas, inventions, and opportunities to be capable, the quality of competence is compelling.

Competence is uniquely individual, built over a lifetime through education, experience, observation, and experimentation. It begins with our first discoveries as small children and continues through old age. There's no way to get it all or fill it full while we are still alive. No series of college degrees or specialized credentials guarantees a maximum competence fulfillment. As Thomas Sowell, a prolific writer, said, "It takes considerable knowledge just to realize the extent of your own ignorance."

The inputs of competence building are not always positive. In fact, most people will tell you that the greatest lessons they've learned are directly related to difficult or painful experiences. For some reason, when something hurts and impresses, the lessons stick.

As a kid, I once watched a guide build a campfire. His method was pretty mundane—sticks, paper, and matches, as opposed to the more dramatic method of striking flint to create sparks. I remember thinking it looked pretty easy. I remember, too, the scorched fingers and wrists I experienced during my own first attempt to build a fire. My sticks were too thick, my paper too loosely bunched, my matches too short. The impressions stuck.

I also recollect learning how flammable human hair is. At Christmastime one year, I leaned down to smell one of the candles my mother had lit in the living room. It had the pleasant, pungent, tangy sweet smell of pine trees. Until, that is, my long hair caught the tip of the flame, and the blaze raced up toward my face. As I ran gasping to the kitchen to douse my hair with water, I felt sick with terror of the fire so near my face and horror at the thought of searing my long tresses. As I soaked my charred hair, I gleaned that leaning over burning candles is a dumb thing to do.

Difficult, even painful, lessons are part of building competence at work, too. Karen, a Fortune 500 vice president, is candid about her lack of finesse in firing her first assistant:

> I was a junior exec—a first-time manager of a part-time employee. My new assistant had been hired by my boss to help me through an unusually busy and chaotic seasonal spike, and her tasks were primarily clerical.
>
> The woman drove me nuts! She was hyperactive, fussy in every detail, and riddled with quirky, jerky mannerisms that made me twitch every time she came near me. Furthermore, with each new task, she insisted on verifying every detail with me—yes, the "M" files go into the "M-N-R" file drawer—and when she had finished, she wanted me to check all of her work to acknowledge that she had done it properly.
>
> As a new manager, what did I know? She wanted to do a good job; I wanted to help her. My boss had entrusted me with the responsibility; I wanted to prove myself worthy.
>
> Fortunately, I am patient by nature, and I have a decent sense of humor. Within a few weeks, my new assistant had gained some confidence. Then she got helpful.

Karen chuckled ruefully at this remark.

She began analyzing our methods and systems of organizing things and decided that there were a few things we could change to improve them. She also had numerous recommendations for reassigning tasks to others.

The woman lasted about two months. During her brief stay, I went to my boss several times asking for help in supervising her. His reply each time was the same, "You wanted help, I got you help. Make the best of it."

When I finally told him she had to go, he told me to carefully detail the reasons why she was unfit for the job. He also told me that I would have to fire her.

At this point, Karen says, she hesitated. But she realized that the assistant was more a hindrance than a help, so she went ahead with the termination. Her story continues:

During the termination meeting, the woman got hysterical. She demanded to know, first of all, why I was firing her when my boss had hired her. I explained that he had given me the responsibility for monitoring and managing her performance. I then went on to explain how the results she was able to attain fell short of what we needed. I did my best to limit my comments to results and the skills required to succeed, while she tried to recast my remarks as personal judgments and attacks. She worked herself into quite a frenzy.

At my wit's end and near panic myself after an hour of mental arm wrestling, I flatly told her that my decision was final. I asked her to leave and come back the next day for her belongings.

That evening, she called my boss at home with an emotional plea for a second chance. He called me, I said no, and the next day, I had another hour-long session with the woman before she finally packed and left. I was shaken for weeks.

In hindsight, this successful executive says she learned a number of valuable management lessons and competencies. "I learned that if you will be responsible for managing someone, even in a team-based, shared-authority environment, you need to be involved in the hiring process. I learned that ongoing feedback is critical. Saving up bad news and dumping it on someone when you've reached the end of your rope is a bad strategy. I learned that it's best to deal with a problem sooner rather than later. And I learned that personal likes and dislikes should be acknowledged—

to yourself, of course—but that job results are the only basis for objectively evaluating someone else's work."

To build a stronger and more resilient backbone, competence must be actively enhanced. Lessons are learned and competence is built only when you take time to reflect on what happened and why. In the campfire instance, I knew only after talking things over with more competent fire builders that my sticks, paper, and matches had each contained flaws that in combination had served to light *me* afire. The candle incident taught me that distance is an excellent thing to keep between hair and flame and that candle snuffers are handy little devices. As for the early workplace experience, Karen says the lessons remain with her to this day.

Successful people actively seek new experiences, new material for learning, and new engagements with other people, events, and problems. They are not necessarily intent on building backbone; this happens as a result of new learning. But if you are intent on strengthening your backbone, building competence is the first place to start.

Which competencies should you develop? That depends on what you want to do with your career and where you happen to be at the moment. We'll explore this in greater detail later. For now, recognize that competence is a fundamental element of backbone. Without competence, you won't be able to stand up or speak out because you won't know what you're standing for or speaking about.

Confidence

The second major component of backbone is confidence. As your competence grows, you'll find yourself becoming more confident. If you doubt this, think about some tasks you do today, routinely, that you wouldn't have thought you were capable of doing a short while ago.

Jill is a team leader in a small architectural consulting firm. Her team is responsible for helping clients reconfigure office space to improve business processes as well as communications. Jill is introverted and quiet. Never in a million years did she think she'd hold a leadership position, especially one that requires so much time in front of others, speaking and teaching. While she says she will probably never be comfortable giving presentations per se, when she can zero in on the client's problem and discuss why the solution her team proposed is the right one, her self-consciousness fades away. She is amazed at her ability to direct people, but she says she is now so used to doing it that she doesn't think twice. Her competence has grown to a level that richly bolsters her confidence.

Jim is the owner, general manager, and chief repair technician of a fast-growing computer company in a small midwestern town. He runs his shop with the help of his wife and a couple of part-timers, and he does most of the field repair work himself. As Jim's business has grown, he has come in contact with a growing number of computer brands, an amazing assortment of system and software ailments, and an unbelievably broad spectrum of human behaviors.

The mechanics of the job come easily to Jim—he had worked for years at one of the largest computer retailers in the area and had earned all kinds of technical certifications—but the people part of the business threw him for a loop. This was especially true when folks became unreasonable in their demands for an immediate resolution of their problem, a ridiculously low price for a repair, or detailed explanations of why their computer broke down at a crucial time. In Jim's mind, computers simply worked until something crashed, and then they either could be fixed or couldn't be fixed. The cosmic reasons for all of this were beyond him, and he found dealing with people both frustrating and time-consuming.

He used to get mad at people who disagreed with his assessment of a repair need. When they challenged him, he felt personally insulted. Sometimes, when they were really nasty (*insistent* is the word he uses now), he would simply tell them he couldn't help them. Life is too short to deal with jerks, he figured. However, he quickly realized that this was not the way to build his business.

Jim shakes his head now in amused satisfaction as he admits that in the ten years he has run his business, his customers have given him the most personal satisfaction. He is at ease with people now, and he enjoys keeping up with the technical advances throughout the computer industry. New knowledge gives him something to brag to his customers about, he says. And brag he does. Jim's competence in the mechanics of his job helped him build both competence and confidence in managing the human side of it, too.

Regardless of what your expertise is, you can undoubtedly look back a few years and appreciate skills you've acquired. Whether it's writing a report, giving a speech, developing a strategy, creating a new invention, evaluating someone's performance, or generally using your business tools with greater deftness, you have developed competence that you didn't have a while ago. This mastery gives you reason to feel better about your ability to contribute at work. That good feeling is confidence.

One of the best confidence-building exercises is to make a list of all of your abilities. Start with basics, though it will feel silly to include items like "wake up in the morning" and "eat pizza for lunch without wearing the evidence for the rest of the day." Think about all the roles you play at work, at home, with friends, and with family. List your skills, giving special note to anything you do uniquely well. Maybe you're able to gather, distill, and interpret massive quantities of data better than most. Maybe you see stories in numbers, thus giving you the ability to add depth and meaning to dry financial statements. Perhaps you keep your head when everyone else panics over a mistake at work. Maybe you listen better than most, so you capture the subtleties of meaning in what your subordinates tell you about a controversial matter. Maybe you're an organizer; maybe you're a dreamer.

Whether you lead, follow, sing, dance, drive, or ride shotgun, your unique competencies provide reason to be confident. Take time to internalize this. You worked for your skills; you deserve the inner strength you feel as a result of your mastery. Your confidence is a source of distinction as you compete with others for power, influence, and recognition at work.

But there's another aspect of confidence of which you need to be aware. Sometimes what appears to be self-confidence isn't. You probably know someone who gives the impression of enormous self-confidence through a commanding voice, squared shoulders, and a brilliant smile. You've probably also had the strange feeling on occasion that something about the outward signals didn't quite match the words and manner. Rather than strength and confidence, the effect came across as superficial, insincere, or unfounded bravado. Eddie Haskell of *Leave It to Beaver* is the archetypal example.

Another example is the facile consultant whose job it is to convince you that he is supremely competent. You see confident body posture and an easy manner of friendliness and helpfulness. You hear impressive words— big ideas and an even bigger vocabulary. But wait.

What is he saying? Are all those big words chained together for a purpose? Is there real thought being conveyed here? Or is it mumbo jumbo delivered at a high rate of speed with the express purpose of creating an impression of unassailable competence?

Dr. Laurence J. Peter, author of *The Peter Principle*, portrays a hilarious scenario in his book as he lays out three columns of words and labels them Column A, Column B, and Column C. The words in each column are big—multisyllabic and sophisticated in meaning. His tongue-in-cheek advice for folks who seek to dazzle others with their brilliance is to select one word from each column, string them together into a sentence, and deliver it with style, energy, and of course a straight face.

What I'm getting at is that sometimes what looks like solid self-confidence is, upon closer inspection, an attempt to conceal a *lack* of confidence. Insecurity is a fact of life for all of us, and to try to deny our unique insecurities usually makes them more visible. It certainly gives them greater control over our emotions and reactions. Why do I mention this? So you won't be cowed by these folks.

When I suggest that strengthening competence is a means of also building confidence, I'm talking about the comfort and sense of mastery that come with learning. The confidence that results from learning will not necessarily make you more comfortable speaking in a crowd or leading the pack. It will, however, provide a deeper feeling of security and stability. You'll begin to realize that you know what you know and are proud of it.

At the same time, as you begin to learn more, it's not unusual to start appreciating the vast shorelines of ignorance that stare back at you. Brain researchers tell us that we use only a minuscule portion of our brains. For many years, this portion was estimated at 10 percent. More recently, the active use of our brains has been estimated at one-1,000th of our capabilities. Imagine that! Imagine the competence you could build if you'd call into service the incredible unused portions of your brain. Imagine the confidence that would ensue. Imagine the power to create, to change, to improve things! Oh, but there's one more element of backbone that you need to develop, and it's a big one.

Risk Taking

The third portion of backbone is risk taking, the ability to engage in intelligent, purposeful ventures on behalf of your career and your company. This may strike you as odd, especially if you consider that many people avoid taking risks as a safe and certain way to learn. Removing potential threats does, after all, allow you to relax a bit and concentrate on learning the task at hand.

But much of your learning arises from your environment—from the situations in which you find yourself, from the people with whom you interact, from the responses you are pressured to give. Nowhere is this truer than at work.

Paul leads an interactive technology group at a midwestern advertising agency. He is responsible for helping clients build their brands through interactive strategies designed to complement traditional marketing efforts. The field, though relatively new, is growing at lightning speed, and research is compiled almost by the hour. Experts of an amazing ilk populate the interactive arena, and companies who choose to get involved understand that risk is inherent.

For Paul, the greatest risk lies in promising a client something that does not play out as expected.

He cites the case of a large Canadian printing company that, several years ago, wanted to be first to offer on-line document-editing capabilities to its business customers. Though this business application was outside the realm of what Paul's group normally undertook, the prospect was exciting. It was also new enough that if the group's results didn't quite match their vision, at least they would have created a functional application that could be enhanced in the future.

Paul conducted worldwide research and found a couple of major corporations that had experimented with systems that enabled document sharing and in-house, on-line editing functions. Adapting portions of several existing software programs and writing supplementary code within his technology group, Paul presented a preliminary version of his software to the Canadian firm.

The reaction of the Canadian executives confounded Paul and his crew. Several of the executives were clearly alarmed at the limitations of the system and openly critical of its "amateurism." Others were staunchly defensive, arguing that as an initial cut at a leading-edge application, the work was well done.

Ultimately, the project was tabled, and Paul was left to ponder the outcome of his risk. Several members of his group felt that they had unfairly suffered a black eye because the client reps didn't know what they wanted. Paul realizes that in his business this is the norm. He decided that the risk had been worthwhile. He had learned a great deal about what applications were being developed; his people had been challenged as they wrote innovative code.

The reaction of his client taught Paul to ask as many specific questions as possible in the development phase of a project, and to feed back the information being supplied to him, verifying at every stage that he and his colleagues were headed in the right direction and that the client's expectations were being met. More important, Paul understood with greater clarity how questions and feedback would serve to set and manage the client's expectations throughout the project. (He also recognized his own reticence in asking questions. Though the field was new and few people had any substantial expertise, he was afraid of appearing less accomplished than he is.)

Too many tabled projects can make you second-guess yourself. That's when risk aversion sets in. Be conscious of this, and guard against it! People with backbone take their lumps, feel the twinges of disappointment or embarrassment, and keep going. If they find over time that they're more bogged than sparked, they seek something else to do.

Keep in mind, too, that one person's risk is another person's routine. For some people, asking a question in itself is a risk. For others, asking isn't a problem, but in a highly visible situation, the nature of the question may take on substantial risk. Understanding the different settings is part of building competence.

Making eye contact is a risky undertaking for some. Taking notes in an obvious manner feels risky to others. Speaking up is tough for many, but doing so is mandatory if our businesses are to meet and survive a host of uncomfortable challenges.

Many department managers, team leaders, and division heads confront an amazing array of risks every working day. From personnel decisions to financial commitments, from strategy setting to selecting a technology platform, from approving special projects to limiting the downside of a spin-off, meeting challenges requires making risk-laden choices.

Should Leona or Leroy be eliminated from the overstaffed department, and what are the potential discrimination liabilities associated with this decision? What are the investment priorities of the firm, and what opportunity costs are associated with them? Should the firm pursue an aggressive E-commerce strategy, or hold fast to a traditional business model until the E-world quiets down? Should the firm investigate innovative benefits in an effort to attract and retain the best talent, or offer a standard package to control escalating human resources costs?

Let's bring it closer to home. Should you offer your research when it directly contradicts an assumption held by someone higher up? Should you tell your boss what you know about the personal hardships of someone who is under fire for making bad decisions? Should you pass along information about a competitor to someone in your company who has attacked you in the past but who will fail badly without it? And if he fails, what are the ramifications for the company? Should you pursue an advanced degree even though your company doesn't offer tuition reimbursement, or shop for another employer who will pay? Should you blow the whistle on a workplace harasser, or turn a blind eye to the matter?

For each of these questions, a vast sea of alternatives lies between the either and the or. Ambiguity is an almost overwhelming reality in business today, and an element of risk is involved in every decision. Backbone is a prized commodity and growing more valuable every chaotic day.

Glenn R. Jones, in an essay entitled "Creating a Leadership Organization with a Learning Mission," writes, "Finding responsible but willing risk takers is one of the greatest challenges for corporate leaders. No matter who the architects of a blueprint are or what the noblesse oblige is of those who will employ it, leadership organizations will be hard-pressed to succeed if they do not have risk takers at all levels who contribute to the design and feel a passionate stake in it." The ability to take intelligent, considered risks comes from understanding a situation, anticipating the effects of your decision on others, correctly estimating the support or opposition for a particular position, carefully considering your own ability to deal with mistakes or failure, and then making a decision in light of all known aspects.

Some of your called shots will be terrific; some will be horrific. Risk taking, by definition, involves a measure of winning and losing. How well you can deal with loss will depend to a great extent on your confidence in approaching each situation. Intelligence and purposefulness do not guarantee fail-safe risk taking. They do, however, enable you to select those risks that have a greater chance of yielding positive results.

In his essay "The Seven Rs of Self-Esteem," Deepak Sethi writes, "Men and women who have high self-esteem are more likely to be intelligent risk takers than those who are less inclined to trust themselves, and the willingness to take appropriate risks itself reinforces self-esteem. The organization of the future, in encouraging risk taking and accepting mistakes as normal, will at once be nurturing self-esteem and inspiring innovation."

Competence—skills built over time and with practice—plus confidence—the self-assurance that comes with mastering skills—equals the ability to take purposeful risk. Successful risk taking underscores competence and enhances confidence. In an upward spiral, the three elements of backbone reinforce one another.

Building a stronger backbone will not necessarily enable you to take risks faster or to feel less stress when important risks come knocking. What it will do is enable you to take the time you need to consider the situation and its options, to fend off those who will press you to a hurried and possibly ill-considered end, and to stand firm when you've made a determination. As important, a strong and healthy backbone will help others feel comfortable with your deliberation and your decision. They will be more likely to carry out the decisions you make, which portends a much better chance of success and satisfaction for all.

Backbone Function

People who have backbone speak their minds, think independently, fear no opposition, can be trusted for their honesty, can take a and hold it, and can tell others what their position is and why. This is a strong model for a successful businessperson.

On the other hand, people who lack backbone rarely speak up; they check the ideas and opinions of (many) others before (maybe) forming their own, fear opposition, and don't tell the truth with any regularity because it changes. These spineless folks can nevertheless be accomplished turf warriors and empire builders, changing their views to align with whoever holds power at the moment, so the challenge to productive and profitable business is clear.

A strong and healthy backbone enables individuals to take as much time as they need to question, consider, and understand; to say what they think because they know what that is; to extend courtesy because they are comfortable in their own skin; to wait in line; to step up to a challenge; and to be who they are with pride and dignity and grace.

It's not just a matter of style. People with backbone come in all personality varieties. Some are loud; some are quiet. Some are articulate; some stumble for words. Some twinkle; some look sleepy. Some are old; some are young. Some are highly educated; some more humble. There are no two backbones alike, but we get a very distinct impression whenever we encounter a person with backbone.

We're likely to sense self-assurance, peacefulness, focused positive energy, attentiveness, courtesy, authenticity, genuineness. People with backbone often radiate a joy at being one of a kind.

Mark is a medical technician at a small community hospital, where several of the doctors like to throw their weight around. They bark orders, throw charts, and in a variety of ways demonstrate to lower-level workers who's boss. Instead of being intimidated or angered by this behavior, as some of his associates are, Mark makes a game of working with the docs. He catches charts on the fly, playfully salutes in response to gruff commands, and smiles tolerantly when they spew off offensive remarks.

Mark projects stability. His coworkers recognize this and are drawn to him because he's not typically reactive. He listens well, speaks with purpose, and makes decisions in which he believes. He can be the voice of reason or play the devil's advocate. In either case, he understands the objective of a situation and works to fulfill it.

People with strong backbone generally have high energy levels, though this energy may not be manifested outwardly. Some move quickly; some don't. Some appear to be very quiet, but you know they are thinking deeply when they express themselves with a strong sense of conviction. Gary, a public relations expert, radiates energy and certainty when he responds to contentious questions with a direct gaze, a well-modulated voice, and a clearly articulated answer. Reporters rarely challenge him because they know that he understands what he's doing and he means what he says.

A healthy sense of humor is another unmistakable mark of backbone; it's often of the self-depreciating kind that enables strong people to take their work seriously and themselves with a grain of salt.

People with backbone know what they think. They may or may not be eloquent, but they are not likely to be wishy-washy. They listen, ask questions, check their own value systems, look at the big picture, understand interdependent elements, and anticipate how their positions impact other functions. They make decisions about what to do or say and stand firm once they've made up their minds. In confidence, they draw upon their ever-expanding competence to take the risks required to move ahead. These and other qualities signal backbone, and we know it, viscerally, when we experience it.

We know it just as surely when it's lacking. We know it when we can't seem to get straight answers, when people won't look us in the eye, when they squirm or mumble or fidget. All these actions convey discomfort at some level and stir within us mirror feelings of discomfort and unease. We don't trust these situations, and we may learn to distrust the individuals involved. We are skeptical of decisions made in these instances, and we begin to take a wait-and-see attitude toward them.

People who don't have a backbone are the ones who sit in silence during meetings and then steam later because they don't like the decisions that were made. These are the people who will argue after the fact but won't volunteer an opinion during a debate. People without a backbone attack others behind the scenes. They whine about unfairness and abuse. They call people names but usually only when they're in a crowd of others who lack backbone.

People who don't have a backbone often write memos instead of facing others straight on. They're afraid of what they'll hear and of their own inability to respond. Many backboneless ones are good at cataloging reasons why decisions should have been different. After the fact. They also have the uncanny ability to run from these reasons if they are challenged. They fear taking a stand, never knowing who will disagree or be upset by a viewpoint.

Some insist that they are being pragmatic. They confess that they wait to see which way the wind is blowing before they say anything in order to hang on to their jobs. While this reticence is understandable, it's a bad strategy if a strong, competitive business is the goal.

Frequently, lack of backbone will declare itself with braggadocio, brashness, rudeness, dominance, self-centeredness, competitiveness for personal gain, inattentiveness, and all sorts of posturing, posing, and crafting of image. You must be alert, however; the differences between backbone and its opposite can be subtle.

Larry is a senior production manager in a privately held distributor of air handling products and systems. The company ranks third in market share in its region and has grown rapidly in recent years. Over the past six months, Larry has noticed a gradual but definite decline in his group's productivity that will soon impact the firm's profitability and may also erode market share. After conducting some research and giving careful thought to the situation, Larry comes up with what appears to be a viable solution. He shares both his problem and his solution in a meeting with his peer executives and asks for their support.

These peers are not involved in Larry's area, don't understand the problem in the same way he does, and haven't studied the circumstances to the extent that he has. They don't feel qualified to pass judgment on the proposed effort. Most are preoccupied with problems of their own, but they support organizational efforts to foster an atmosphere of empowerment and autonomy. Thus, as long as they feel that Larry's solution will not impinge on their work (or their bonuses), they give the nod to proceed. Or, perhaps more accurately, they don't comment one way or another, and Larry takes silence to mean concurrence.

Herein lies a problem.

Two guys in the group know with certainty that what Larry wants to do will require adjustments in the daily work habits of people in other areas. One of these areas is run by a woman who takes pride in her department's efficiency. She knows how much profit she generates per employee and is not the least bit interested in hearing about changing anything. She has made herself clear on this point in the past and has effectively stonewalled all previous change efforts.

Past attempts to persuade, cajole, or force the woman to alter her department's operations have led to unpleasant exchanges that resulted in stony silences and an emotionally charged atmosphere for weeks afterward. People learned that it's easier to leave her alone than to engage her in any discussion about change or improvement. In Larry's situation, the two guys knew she would eventually be affected and would rear her ugly head in protest, but they chose not to bring it up. They simply hoped for the best. No backbone here.

Another guy in the room during the presentation doesn't think Larry realizes how poor morale is within Larry's own group. He is wary that Larry's idea to implement changes will further frustrate Larry's own workers and ultimately lead to the defection of several of them. This man is unsure how to present his apprehensions and decides that this meeting is not the right place or time. He doesn't want to precipitate an inappropriate discussion about the pros and cons of Larry's management style, so he, too, keeps mum. Nice guy. No backbone.

Still another person knows of significant initiatives soon to be announced that will impact Larry's proposed solution. But because these initiatives have to date been discussed only in private sessions with those immediately responsible, the woman does not feel authorized to mention them. Questionable backbone. If she were to pull Larry aside and mention that change is in the wind, then perhaps backbone can be discerned.

If Larry had a strong backbone himself, he would know that something isn't quite right. The overall lack of response, the noncommittal shrugs, and the eerie quiet that engulfs the room as he asks for support are signals. He should explore them, but he is so eager to start his project that he doesn't want to waste time debating something that nobody else knows or cares much about. (This is a common reaction and one that is staunchly defended on the basis of moving things along.)

On the surface, all this appears benign, even positive. Larry has discovered a problem, proposed a solution, and expressed his eagerness to implement it. His peers have agreed—some by default—to allow him to proceed. Energized and proud of his win, Larry announces the solution to his work group with enthusiasm and energy. The group captures his excitement, and together they get started on implementation.

But before long, effects of the solution begin to impact other departments. The ripple effect kicks in, and now Larry's peers become interested. Quirks develop that were not anticipated. Operations that once ran smoothly begin to falter. People outside of Larry's department begin to get materials from Larry's group that look or behave differently from the way they have in the past and are unhappy about this. Nobody told them about the changes that Larry made. Nobody told them they'd be affected and would have to revise their operations because of something Larry did. Frankly, it looks as though nobody thought processes through to foresee the implications of Larry's work or the adjustments that might be needed.

The energy and enthusiasm that drove the change effort may now be labeled as naïveté and shortsightedness. Larry's competence may be called into question. His group may suffer large-scale chastisement, and as a result, their early hope dissolves into embarrassment and disillusionment. How soon will this group participate in another improvement effort?

In situations like this, poor communication is often held out as the reason for the effort's failure. If only Larry had communicated more broadly, associates in other departments would have known to expect some changes. Larry may now react defensively, saying his peers should have taken responsibility to notify their own departments. After all, Larry had told them about his plan and asked for their support. How much responsibility can or should he take beyond his own area?

And if Larry had challenged his peers' passivity, he'd have been absolutely right. But he didn't. His faulty backbone precluded him from actively seeking out and removing the barriers that he knew, deep down, were there somewhere. What originally looked like strong backbone (competence in uncovering a problem, confidence in outlining a solution to his peers, and risk taking in going ahead with implementation) wasn't quite. In fact, Larry does have—and did demonstrate—the three elements of backbone. He just didn't trust them enough. He took shortcuts. His competence in figuring out a solution was not matched by competence in articulating or implementing it. Ditto for confidence. He needed help, but he chose not to take the risk of sincerely asking for it.

Faulty backbone frequently combines with organizational confusion and ends up in rationalizations that keep people stuck. In this instance, the management group shrugged off the failed attempt at change. After all, Larry's a good guy with fine intentions. Larry's peers decide to take the organizational high road by forgetting the failure, saluting the effort, and encouraging him to try again. They pat themselves on the back for being part of an innovative and creative problem-solving organization and for standing firm in their determination to support individual empowerment and experimentation.

But they fail to see the disillusionment, the budding cynicism, and the draining of energy that these failed efforts foster. They continue on as if it's no big deal, but there's a nagging sense of unease. They may wonder silently why this solution that looked so practical didn't work. Perhaps some will look more candidly at their own actions and recognize that they could have done something more or different to improve the outcome. They won't admit this to anyone else, but they may see it themselves. Most will hesitate to attempt anything even remotely similar to Larry's botched plan because they don't want to suffer what poor Larry went through. The misgivings quietly build, and before anyone realizes it, Larry's attempt becomes an "undiscussable," a term coined by authors Kathleen D. Ryan and Daniel K. Oestreich in *Driving Fear Out of the Workplace*.

This, by the way, is how cultures get sick in little increments.

How could a stronger backbone have helped Larry? What could he have done differently? He could have gotten a better read on the bigger picture within the organization. Had he done this, he would have been better able to anticipate problems and head them off. He could have acknowledged his own discomfort and taken steps to alleviate his greatest concerns. He could have asked several of his peers for their confidential and candid assessment of his plan. As he kicked off the implementation, he could have been more active in gauging its effects outside his own work group and addressing reservations while they were still small. This troubleshooting may have indicated that a number of adjustments were needed in the original plan.

Each of these steps would have added a measure of competence, which would have bolstered Larry's confidence. Strengthened in this way, he would have been more likely to take the necessary risks to succeed.

Now meet Sandra, a woman with an impressive dossier of accomplishments in her field. She's a thinker, a planner, and a theoretician who has an enormous talent for creating stunning strategic marketing plans and programs. But Sandra lacks the ability to work with others to implement her grand ideas. She's continually frustrated by the seeming ineptitude of her associates, and unfortunately, from time to time, she tells them so. Sandra doesn't explain why or how she came up with a great idea, so people who work with her have little chance to get it. Not much camaraderie happening here.

In fact, Sandra isolates herself in her world, while her associates hunker down in theirs. Their work forces them to spend time together, but it's usually compressed to a minimum weekly team meeting. And this meeting usually feels both pinched and rushed, so the bad vibes get strengthened.

Though a brilliant strategist, Sandra has no understanding of the systems or skills required to implement her visions. In her mind's eye, she can see a program rolling out successfully, but she doesn't know the details of how to make it happen. In defense of herself, she says she hasn't the time to keep up with a wide range of fast-changing tools. The nits and gnats of system and equipment improvements are not her concern, nor are changes made within the supplier network that provides various segments of overall programs. Sandra argues that she has always left the details of finding and managing systems and suppliers to project teams. She knows enough about what's available in a global sense, and she always aims high as a visionary and an innovator. But she isn't knowledgeable enough about the resources directly accessible to make her programs truly effective, doable, or profitable.

Further, she is intimidated by those who do know this stuff. This reaction stems from a bad experience. Earlier in her career, she had tried to explain a new program and the logical steps (as she saw them) involved in creating and implementing it. The people responsible for making the program work quickly realized that her implementation knowledge was limited and began to talk among themselves about how to proceed. Sandra felt that she had lost control of the meeting, allowing it to spin out into a "premature discussion of irrelevant detail." Angry and embarrassed by her own inability to manage both the meeting and the project, she withdrew. She admits that she had felt painfully inadequate and that she decided right then and there that she'd never again expose herself to such embarrassment. To conceal her discomfort, she developed an air of intellectual superiority. And while aloofness served her well in creating this impression, it drove most people away from her. Ultimately, despite her talent, her success was limited; her power and influence were severely constrained.

How would backbone have helped? True backbone would have allowed Sandra to recognize her skills *and* her limitations. It would have helped her understand her need to work with others to fill in the areas in which she falls short. It would have allowed her to make no apology for having limitations, but rather to emphasize the contributions she could make with the skills and knowledge she does have.

Backbone within the implementation group might have allowed someone to patiently explain how successful programs are built. In a mutual sharing of ideas and expertise, the best processes for the program could then be selected and verified. Such cooperation and mutual instruction can occur only when people are comfortable enough with their abilities and positions to assist in an overall group effort.

Healthy backbone all around would change the dynamics and the results for these workers. Sandra could expand her own level of understanding, making her even more competent and productive. Ditto for her associates. As a result of their learning from each other and truly working in tandem, discovery replaces huffy isolationism. Brilliant strategies get married to kick-butt production. The team wins. Together.

Is backbone important? Hugely.

Why Is Backbone Important?

Backbone is important because without it, we fail. If we simply continue to show up at work, sit in on the various meetings we've scheduled, engage our brains only occasionally, and feel vaguely uneasy about the direction in which we're headed, I submit to you that the direction is marked "extinction."

Why do companies spend so much time and money dealing with consultants instead of working with their own people? Why do strategic plans so often end up shelved?

Why do so many inadequate workers not only keep their jobs but get regular pay increases besides? Why do so many young people demand and get huge initial salaries?

Why do so many people leave meetings and think to themselves, "I wish I had said (fill in the blank)"? Why are so many people angry at having to work with disruptive, negative colleagues?

Why are so many companies shackled by the past? When new agendas are set, why are they so often ignored or downplayed?

Complete answers to all of these whys can be found in the myriad management books available at your local or dotcom bookstore. I will contend that one fundamental answer will suffice: Someone (everyone?) involved in each of these situations lacks backbone.

> **The next decade will be full of opportunities for those who are willing to challenge themselves, to learn, to share, and to change. Those who resist change will be left behind and will totally miss the excitement of creating the future.**
>
> C.K. PRAHALAD, CO-AUTHOR, *COMPETING FOR THE FUTURE*

Several years ago, I talked to a nationwide sample of CEOs and senior executives. I asked questions about leadership and listened closely. I knew that corporate execs would be well versed in the theory of leadership and power; I wanted to see how it played out in real life.

What I heard sent a chill through me and left me with a sense of foreboding. What I heard crystallized my belief that business is in serious trouble. I heard a clarion call for focus and discipline, for the ability to see the big picture and think things through. I heard a plea for backbone.

These comments are from the president of a public relations firm:

> I would be afraid to answer some of these questions. I wouldn't put them in writing. I'd give you what I think my boss wants to hear. I'd certainly want to know what my boss thinks of this whole thing.
>
> Your question asking me if I feel I'd been properly prepared prior to assuming my executive position is abrasive and threatening. I wouldn't admit to not being properly trained, at least not in writing. I might tell you that if we were talking privately, but I wouldn't want my boss to know that.

Rick, a department head in a major automotive company, went further:

> Do we have a problem with leadership? I think the problem boils down to the fact that these guys don't have the information or the balls to do the right thing. We have lots of discussions around here, but nobody really wants to change things. It's too hard. It's too confusing. There's too much involved.

Excuses, excuses.

> You sit in meetings all day talking about who you are and what you do and how you're going to make money. And everybody in the room sees things a little differently and they absolutely know what the right answer is.
>
> If there's something we're really good at, it's getting everybody's input without letting anyone be too rude or too honest. We let people make really smart comments, and we all feel good about these smart people we work with. But when it's all said and done, the customer doesn't care. And the fact is that when customers have a dollar or a thousand dollars to spend, we need to be talking to them about things they care about and building a level of trust that will convince them to give us their money instead of giving it to our competitor. It sounds simple, but in fact, a lot of stuff gets in the way.

What gets in the way? Plenty. Opinions based on little more than personal experience and limited query. Disagreements about what the business is, who should be in charge of what, what customers want, how much they're willing to pay, who the competitors are, and what factors outside the company impact success. Fear. Fear of being wrong, making a mistake, losing a job. Change. New systems, new management ideas, new tools, new workers. Tradition. Inertia. Uncertainty.

What are the stakes? According to Rick:

> I think you have to do everything in business recognizing that you are part of a relationship. If you do the wrong things enough times, the relationship will be destroyed, and it won't matter whether your competitor has talked to your customer or not. The customer will go looking for a provider that will keep its promise. That promise may relate to convenience, a bargain price, outstanding service, or what have you. And the nature of your promise becomes the premise for your business.
>
> It sounds so simple, and it should be. But we've got a lot of guys around here who just don't have the guts to focus. Somehow it's easier to insist on getting a report and blaming somebody for screwing it up than to sit down, think, and really figure this thing out.
>
> Then, when it's figured out, we have to do something about it. That gets scary. And everyone waits to see who's going to do something first. Because if someone else does something and then gets criticized or ridiculed or shot, then everybody else is glad not to have been involved. They all go back to their offices and thank God it didn't happen to them. They learn to be very careful not to rock the boat.
>
> You can see all the traps. Bottom line is that for most of us, if things are going along OK, we're reluctant to make waves. We don't want to lose our jobs, and we don't really have clear answers; we just have nagging feelings that situations could be better. We keep wanting our leaders to do something impressive to restore our energies and attitudes.
>
> We all recognize that when you change patterns, especially at the top, it takes time for the pieces to settle down, for the gears to mesh again, and for the whole system to get moving again. We understand that, but we don't have the patience to stay with it. We look at quarterly financial results and change people or systems or processes to improve the results for next quarter. When the next quarterly results suggest tinkering in another area, we're off tinkering.
>
> It's a difficult, dangerous cycle. And I think part of the problem is that people are not brave enough to take a stand and stick with it.

What do you suppose would happen if folks learned how to be brave enough to take a stand and stick with it? What would happen if men and women became actively engaged in their businesses and acted on purpose? Chances are good that we'd have better and more productive companies, better relationships, and more fun.

Still, leaders demonstrate ambivalence when it comes to having an entire workforce develop backbone. A friend of mine who owns several small businesses and is adept at finding new opportunities and making them grow said, "Of course I want people who know what they're doing and can take responsibility for things, but I sure don't want a bunch of young punks with attitude."

I have heard this same concern at other times and in other places. Incidentally, younger folks have told me they don't want a bunch of old farts with attitude either.

Given the widespread—some might say global—hesitancy to rock the boat, take a stand, or otherwise leave the beaten path, I don't think an attitude epidemic is anything to worry about.

The Cost of Missing Backbone

"If you're not part of the solution, you're part of the problem." How many times have you heard that? But what if you don't understand the problem? Now you've got serious trouble.

Here's the problem. A missing or weak backbone causes ideas to be lost, thoughts to go unspoken, frustrations to pile up, and consensus building to become a core competency.

Compete for the future, you say? Forget about it. Manage for the future? Foster leadership? Champion empowerment? You laugh. There is an ocean of scorn building for what really are good and useful ideas. But popular management theories fall flat when the people who could make them soar (that's you) don't have the gumption to dig in and do the hard and scary work of changing things. A healthy backbone would help.

Look at such problems as turnover, escalating consulting fees, aborted change efforts, the costs of correcting faulty workmanship, and any number of other quantifiable aspects of corporate restructuring. Lots of disgruntled workers like to point to inept management as the reason for so much corporate waste. But ask yourself how much more you could do. How much better would things be if you were to say what you really think instead of nodding in agreement and choking back your scorn?

What if you took time to understand what's going on instead of assuming that what was true for the old-line leaders is still true with the new guys? What if you really tried to straighten something out instead of throwing in the towel and moving on to another company?

Frederick F. Reichheld, in his 1996 book *The Loyalty Effect*, presents chilling statistics. Customers are defecting at a rate of 10 to 30 percent per year; employee turnover rates of 15 to 25 percent are common; average annual investor churn exceeds 50 percent per year. The costs to business are huge.

> **I have spoken up at previous jobs and at my current job. A few times, I was unable to get the support I needed, so the ideas I advocated died on the vine. Most recently, I seem to have people who agree with me in private but don't voice their support in public. So, nothing has happened except my getting frustrated. Personally, I never feel comfortable speaking up. I find it hard to believe that I'm absolutely right and everyone else is absolutely wrong. I prefer to solicit a few peers before I go up the chain.**
>
> ANONYMOUS POST TO A WEB
> CONFERENCE BOARD

Data crunchers can crank out reams of similar statistics cataloging all sorts of business waste. But even these attempts to quantify and understand the bottom-line impact miss the point. The high cost of missing backbone—deficient competence, flaccid confidence, and an aversion for risk—goes much deeper and has far more pernicious effects than even the broad range of categories we quantify today. Because we can't measure them accurately or represent them concretely on our balance sheets, we tend to dismiss them. Authors Kathleen D. Ryan and Daniel K. Oestreich summarize workplace fear, for example, as negative feelings about organizations and point out that trying to translate these into concrete costs "is like trying to calculate the dollar impact of a dissatisfied customer."

But the fact that we can't determine concrete costs doesn't mean we can continue to turn a blind eye or wring our hands in inefficacy. Literally hundreds of examples of corporate waste are associated with missing backbone. Energy is wasted in guessing games. Strong personalities tend to rule, whether their ideas are best or not. Some good ideas are lost through lack of exposure.

Bad roads are taken; blame is assigned for failed efforts. People in leadership positions fail to exercise authority. Followers of weak leaders are disillusioned. Troublemakers gain momentum when no one chastises them.

Risks are rarely taken. Certainty is revered. Historical wins are projected whether the future looks the same as the past or not. Faulty plans are implemented.

Decision making by consensus yields lackluster performance. Political correctness overtakes business sense. Specialty groups wield excessive power, and resources are allocated disproportionately.

Bad behaviors are propagated while good people get confused, then angry. They leave. Weakness is fostered. Money is wasted. Failures become more commonplace and raise few concerns.

Thinking is stymied. Catatonic behavior takes over. Cultures become sick. Consultants are brought in to fix things. Little progress is made (and sometimes things get even worse).

It's not a pretty picture. And if you've been involved or affected by backboneless situations (who hasn't?), you know how they leave you feeling. Sapped. Disappointed. Maybe even angry.

It's time for a change.

Unintended Competencies

Start at the beginning. If competence is the first element of backbone, is a lack of backbone simply an indication of incompetence? Actually, no. In fact, if practice makes perfect, you've probably developed some competencies that you'd rather not brag about.

There are four that plague almost everyone, and they flourish when we allow discussions to wander, decisions to waver, and all sorts of nonsense to go unchallenged. The big four are avoidance, shuffling the deck, marking time, and the one we use to protect ourselves from feeling awful: rationalization.

Avoidance

This particular competence is everywhere. You know how it goes: Don't feel like calling that cranky coworker? Go on-line instead. Don't want to deal with that report just now? Call your buddy over at XYZ company for an update on yesterday's trade show. Wish you could skip that tough conversation with your problem employee? Talk about sports instead. (It's OK; you're building a relationship.)

We avoid complex or confusing issues by changing the subject when they pop up. We avoid responsibility for getting things done by not sticking with a premise long enough to resolve anything. We avoid hurt feelings by sidestepping or hurrying past difficult situations. We avoid blaming anyone for anything by continuing to allow discussions to wander. We avoid progress, but we also avoid any negative comment about our avoidance by assuring others and ourselves that at the next meeting we'll get something done. "Did you check with Larry on that?" "No, sorry. Did I say I would? I'll give him a call this afternoon and let you know what he says at our next meeting." And so it goes.

Shuffling the Deck

Avoidance enables shuffling the deck. As we avoid one topic, another presents itself. If it, too, is controversial or unclear, we shuffle it back to the bottom of the pile. With a long list of priorities—things that must be done if the business is to survive—there is always a well-stocked deck to shuffle.

Goals change if a stumbling block occurs between the time a goal is set and agreed upon and the time it is scheduled to be completed. Take, for example, a sales tracking and reporting system that one company wants to implement. The company wants a central client information system; salespeople want to keep their own independent files. Management says, "Thou shalt document sales calls"; salespeople say, "In your dreams."

This may seem ridiculous in an age of distributed and shared knowledge, but history plays a dominant role here. The company has grown impressively over its fifty-plus years by letting sales executives run their accounts as they see fit. The salespeople take pride in the way they have built their firm. But time passes, and things change. Tradition meets reality, revealing costs that the company can no longer absorb or ignore.

You can imagine the many discussions involved in this kind of culture-changing mandate from management. Strong feelings tumble out clumsily. Name-calling erupts. Resentments spew all over the place. But in an effort to "evolve the new practices," tough stuff is often shoved to the bottom of the pile. Emotional reactions are smoothed over by a change of topic. Easier topics are dwelt upon so people can calm down and find ways to get through the discord. The deck is shuffled time and time again, and at last report, the new system isn't quite in place yet. This competence is finely tuned, to the detriment of many.

Marking Time

Deck shuffling can lead to the appearance that the status quo is preserved as time rolls by. This is a dangerous fallacy. While procedures appear to be locked in place in internal struggles, outside everything is changing again and again. Over time, internal struggles and the reasons for them become obsolete. So do companies.

The more times a particular subject is discussed without action being taken, the more likely it is that the subject will burn itself out. It's amazing how status quo sneaks in even while we're "focusing" and "having excellent dialogue" about the "issues" of the day. This is one reason why priorities come and go with so little progress noted. John Kotter, in his excellent book *Leading Change*, points to a lack of urgency as a chief reason why companies fail in their change efforts. We don't have the skills to act urgently when we have practiced avoidance, deck shuffling, and marking time so effectively for so long.

Rationalization

Rationalization is the granddaddy of backbone-deficient competencies, as demonstrated by people and organizations every single business day. Pick a subject, ask a question, and listen for the answer.

Here are a few examples of rationalization:

"We can't change the requirements of the job because we'll lose the very people who are currently bringing in all the company's business." (Though by keeping things the way they are now, we can effectively project a date when this company will be out of business.)

"We can't charge a different price because our customers may be pushed into the arms of our competitor." (Though by retaining our pricing structure, we will erode our profitability at a rate of 20 percent per year starting now.)

"We can't introduce a new computer system now—we don't have time to teach people how to use it." (Though by avoiding technological advancement, we assure our inability to compete, to communicate, and to survive.)

"We can't require different reports—no one will know how to read them." (Though the reports we have now give us information that is irrelevant.)

"We fired this person because he finally crossed the line." (But the guy who has crossed the line dozens of times is still here because he has saved this company millions of dollars. And besides, if we fired him, he'd probably sue us. He's a mean SOB.)

In each of these rationalizations, we see defective backbone at work. Whether caused by a shortfall of competence, a lack of confidence, or a refusal to risk, the cost of missing backbone is dear. But we can do better. And we need to do better.

Imagine what would happen if everyone in business would dedicate him- or herself to the building of a strong and healthy backbone. I'll bet we'd be looking at some kind of renaissance for business. And it's high time.

Get the Big Picture

LET'S FACE IT. We operate today in a fast-paced and ambiguous environment in which complex organizations serve a wide variety of client needs. Already intense pressures to satisfy every constituent body including customers, employees, shareholders, and any number of interested stakeholders will continue to increase. A while back, in anticipation of this growing complexity and pressure, specialization boomed. Just ten years ago, workers were advised to select a specialty, hone it to high levels of expertise, and use it as a competitive wedge to get ahead. Now we're seeing that this touted specialization, and its attendant compartmentalization of work groups, doesn't serve us as well as we expected it to.

As a result, we're forming teams, championing democratic leadership, and encouraging workers at all levels to broaden their knowledge and expertise. Take heed: strategic capabilities are important. And even if the pendulum swings back toward specialization some day, a big-picture understanding of your organization, industry, and global environment will stand you in excellent stead.

> **In an age of discontinuities, the capacity to conceptualize and synthesize the whole, to see the connections between parts and be able to imagine the future, can be crucial.**
>
> C. K. PRAHALAD, CO-AUTHOR, *COMPETING FOR THE FUTURE*

At this point in your career, you may have exceptional command of your area of expertise. You may even have an excellent knowledge of how your work group plugs in to a larger domain both locally and globally.

Many outstanding executives have tremendous experience and vision with regard to their functional areas, such as marketing or logistics or information technology. Some are highly decorated with industry awards. Some become noted experts who speak routinely at large conferences. Truthfully, most managers would love that kind of acknowledgment and notoriety.

But a more compelling question for today and the future is: How conversant are you with all the aspects of your company? How strategic is your outlook and your thinking?

Generally speaking, when you concentrate hard on winning in your area of expertise, you have little reason to interact substantially with certain other areas of your company. You'll typically understand the role of people whose work influences yours in some way, and you may have reason to come in contact with others on a troubleshooting basis, but it's not at all uncommon to work for years in an organization and never meet many of the other employees. Traditionally, workers were not encouraged to move around much or to gain in-depth knowledge about the company. Managers were more concerned with employees' doing the best job they could in the positions for which they were hired, and leaving others alone to do the same. After all, bonuses frequently depended upon the success of one's unit. Perhaps this is still the way things work in your organization. It is for many.

But we're beginning to understand the folly of this approach. Peter Senge's 1995 groundbreaking book *The Fifth Discipline: The Art & Practice of the Learning Organization* sensitized business leaders to the importance of systems thinking and integrated learning. This insight was timely, as we quickly became connected to others through technology in a bigger, faster, and much more complex world. In the fall of 1998 in an article written for *Strategies & Business* magazine, Charles Handy detailed the morale-deadening aspects of limiting worker involvement to their specialized tasks. He stated: "The micro-division of labor has fostered a basic mistrust of human beings. People weren't allowed to put the whole puzzle together. Instead they were given small parts because companies feared what people would do if they knew and saw the whole puzzle. Human assets shouldn't be misused. Brains are becoming the core of organizations—other activities can be contracted out."

Most forward-thinking businesspeople agree. Still, broadening your awareness and appreciating the importance of integration—developing your strategic skills—mean that an already lengthy list of challenges is expanded. How are you to amplify your understanding of your organization while deftly managing a multitude of daily demands? Pressures to perform well in your area may allow little time for broad-scale reflection.

Know the Pieces

One excellent way to begin expanding your knowledge is to construct a "big-picture map" of your organization. The big picture will show you what your organization looks like in context. It will depict major segments of your business, including important connections and interactions with others. It should include size and scope indicators, geographic locations, and other identifiers. When completed, the big picture will clearly show where you are in relationship to the whole.

Begin by indicating the location of your desk in relationship to your internal work group, whether that's a department, a team within a department, a desk within a bullpen, or whatever your situation entails. Work outward from there, identifying the major functional areas/departments/workgroups/teams within your company. Admittedly, this will be easier if you happen to work for a fairly structured organization, and it may get awfully confusing if your organization is mostly virtual. No matter. The idea is to map out to the best of your ability what things look like from a big-picture perspective.

Draw large squares for each of the main functioning groupings, and label them. As an aid, see if you can find someone—an operations person, perhaps, or someone in charge of building maintenance—to give you a floor plan or other schematic drawing of the building. This will help you account for all functions and see how they are positioned in relationship to one another. One company I know included such a drawing in an invitation for an open house celebration. Guests appreciated having a pictorial of the building layout and used it to visit the areas of special interest to them.

Many companies have built or are building an intranet—an electronic information and communications network tying all internal elements of an organization together. Companies use intranets to post business news, policies, personnel directories, and announcements; some have gone so far as to post monthy financials for all employees to study and understand.

If your firm has an intranet, it likely includes all operational elements. In this case, your internal big-picture map is right there. If your company has not yet developed an intranet, your compilation of big-picture elements would be an excellent starting point for launching one. (And wouldn't that be a neat project to get credit for?)

Sketch out the pieces that exist, how many there are, and approximately how big they are. You'll want to study the lay of the land, how pieces interact, and what kinds of influences are exerted among and between them.

Start with your organization's headquarters, but remember also to include outlying sales offices, manufacturing or processing facilities, distribution and fulfillment centers, and any other remote facilities. Add the names of point people in each of the functional/department areas and the size of each "local" workforce. Don't be too concerned at this stage about precision; you're drawing a sketch of your company's operations to get a bird's-eye view of what happens where and roughly how many people it involves.

To illustrate, let's pick a firm with a fairly substantial headquarters in the Midwest and sales offices in San Diego, Houston, Philadelphia, and New York. The big-picture map would show the main facility with functional areas delineated and approximately how many people work in each area. Production might include 75 people, customer service 30 people, information systems 45 people, and so on. The outlying offices might be represented by smaller icons, with the number of salespeople written inside. If other sales-related processes such as ordering and customer service are performed at the satellite offices, these would be indicated as well. If any products are handled from these offices or if sales literature or other materials are delivered to them in volume, shipping and receiving would be noted too.

Once you have identified all the areas in which people work internally for your organization, expand your map by including everyone outside the firm with an involvement in your work. Include customers, suppliers, bankers, regulators, board members, business partners, government agencies, consultants, trade associations, and schools from which you hire interns. How can you possibly know all these? Ask others within your organization about their outside relationships. Pay attention to names of people to whom others refer when they talk about their projects. When something gets done in a place other than your organization, you know you have external connections to include on your big-picture map.

These outside connections form corporate extranets. If your company has created one, find out as much about it as you can. But don't limit your map to what your company's extranet includes. Typically, it won't include trade associations, schools from which job candidates are recruited, or certain other entities with which your firm deals on an irregular basis.

Denote connections as external by placing them outside the area of the large squares. A good method for doing this is to add a clear overlay to your original schematic, on which you can show the external groups. As I write this, I am supposing there is an outstanding electronic drawing tool, and it embarrasses me not to be familiar with it. (I'll add researching this to my own list of competence-building activities.) If there is one that can accomplish the task I'm describing here, by all means exploit its best capabilities!

Finally, add all the groups that have an interest in the success or failure of your firm but that don't work directly with it. Families, friends, competitors, providers of special awards, and recipients of the firm's charitable donations are examples. Think of as many associations as you can, and add them to your big-picture map. Give these interested parties special symbols, or add them as a list off to the side or along the bottom. When you're finished, you'll have an extended and entailed drawing showing a wide variety of elements associated with your firm. You'll have the big picture.

You may be thinking now that this is way beyond anything you have either the time or the energy to create. It's a common reaction. It's also why so few people have a good understanding of the scope and size of their organizations. Those who take the time to draft this chart, even in a rudimentary way, have a much broader appreciation for how things work. Their thinking tends to be more sophisticated and their decisions more effective. They have a global vision that fosters backbone. These are the people to whom others listen.

Color the Pieces

Once you get the big pieces in place, you can go back and have some fun adding color to your map. Pull out your favorite neon markers, or borrow the kids' crayons, and literally give the pieces different colors. This will help you see them individually and as elements in the whole. Play with the color schemes. Make the finance group green (you're an optimist) or red (you're a realist). Make the management information systems (MIS) group shocking blue for electricity. Give the creatives a funky fuchsia. When you're done with the markers, get going with words. Add as much information as you can about the elements, "coloring" each with its own shades of personality, power, and effectiveness.

Dave is in charge of marketing. What do you know about marketing? How does work arrive in and depart from the marketing group? (Or does it get stuck?) What special projects is marketing working on? Have they pioneered anything new?

How many people work in the group? How long has each of them been there? How old are they? What's the ratio of men to women? Are they close, an internal family? Do they play well with others? How much power do they wield as a group?

What professional associations do they belong to? What's the current buzz in the industry? What regulations do they worry about? How many conferences or trade shows do they attend each year? Are they into continuing education—I mean lifelong learning? What special awards does the marketing industry hand out? Has anybody in the group won any?

You'll find that as you start recording this kind of information, you'll start wondering about things that never occurred to you before. Let's say, for example, that you heard that marketing was responsible for the introduction of a new Internet strategy a while back. You remember being vaguely impressed, but you didn't give it much thought beyond that. But now that you're thinking about marketing, you wonder how they went about it. How did they figure out what they needed and where to find it? How did they budget for it? With whom did they work internally? Certainly the information systems (IS) people had to be involved at some level. How did that go? Was there conflict? There had to have been. How was it resolved?

When you've recorded as much as you know about the group, start writing down what you know about Dave. What's his background? What special skills does he bring to his job? How long has he been with the company? Who are his friends and allies at work? How extensive is his network outside the organization?

Is he a quick decision maker and doer, or does he like to ponder situations before taking action? How does he prefer to communicate: face-to-face? in writing? electronically? by phone? How do the people who work for and with him respond?

Does he get to meetings on time, or is he a habitual latecomer? Does he appear to be organized or haphazard? Does he harp on the same themes all the time, or does he resolve problems and move on? Is he consistent in these patterns, or do people confront an entirely new guy each day?

Is he well respected within the organization? Are his ideas sound? How good is he at presenting them? How effective is he in getting things done?

You'll find that just as thoughts about one group led you to another, thoughts about Dave will lead you to other people. This becomes time- and mind-consuming, and it's likely that once you get started, you'll be absorbed with questions, ideas, and insights that you never imagined before. For this reason, it's best to work on this project before or after hours in a place where you'll have some privacy and quiet time to think.

A word of advice and caution: Confine your effort to business. Forget about personal details, and eschew gossip of any kind. Remember, your objective in building this bank of knowledge is to increase your own power and influence. If you drift into personal information and begin to ask or speculate about private matters, your credibility as a professional will be shot. You may find lots of folks who would love to gossip with you, and you may delight in how your circle of "friends" grows, but you'll soon be seen as a gossip and a gadabout, not as a serious businessperson.

Connect the Pieces

Now that you have some idea of the number and size of pieces and of the "color" of each, you can connect the dots to form an integrated system. An excellent way to do this is to create critical project paths.

Pick a project with which you're familiar, and draw lines from one department or functional area to another based on how work comes into your firm and how it gets done. Include a floor plan. Show when work is done upstairs or downstairs, in Building One or Building Four, by a group of people gathered in a special area of the company or by many people with "virtual" locations. This is the critical path of a job. It will provide a sense of where materials go and what happens to them. It'll help you understand an overall process flow, making you sensitive to the dynamics of timeliness, accuracy, and dependability between groups and functions.

Again, this will be easier if your organization is fairly structured or if your products and services are fairly standardized and processes are clearly outlined. Where this is not the case, your lines are likely to traverse great expanses and loop back over each other in patterns that would put Etch-A-Sketch or Spirograph drawings to shame. Incidentally, if you've got more squiggles than you can keep track of, some streamlining may be in order.

Depending upon the number and variety of products and services you offer, you'll probably construct several critical paths, maybe many. Ask people around the organization for help, and don't worry about feeling confused. Business is complex today, and representing its flow using drawings can be challenging. But it's a kick when it works.

See if you can draw lines between external entities and the internal groups or functions with which they interact most often. These relationships are important to understand. Think about the kinds of interactions that occur, and label them with different colors or symbols. Note frequency of interaction and whether there is a seasonal or other periodic aspect. Note, too, how frequently the various groups are mentioned during routine conversations and meetings at work. Develop a sensitive ear to comments you hear about these entities (internal and external), and add them to your growing bank of information and knowledge.

With critical project paths completed, see if you can do the same sort of thing with the management team. Start with Dave from marketing, mapping his connections with suppliers, professional associations, charitable groups, regulators, educational bodies, and the like. Don't worry that you're drawing what looks like a huge ball of yarn. The act of individually drawing connections gives you the general sensitivity and insights you're after. The big picture is what you want.

Construction of your big-picture map will give you incredible insights into who and what are important to your organization. You'll begin to recognize the organization's strengths and weaknesses, its areas of success and struggle. You'll see where principals spend most of their time. If you pay close attention, you can gather the same intelligence about business partners, suppliers, and competitors. You're well on your way to becoming a strong strategic thinker.

Beware. You're going to run across people who will be highly suspicious of this research. Some will be jealous of your initiative and will cast it as a personal public relations project—a shameless brown-nosing exercise. Some will think you're aggressively and indelicately pursuing your own career. That's OK. There will be others who will appreciate your efforts and may even be entertained by the notion of charting the business. A new sense of adventure and playfulness may develop, to the benefit of all.

In truth, you *are* working to improve your knowledge in the hope of improving your opportunities and, yes, ultimately to increase your power and influence. The negative thoughts and responses of others are not your concern. Be polite and professional, and keep getting smarter. Be open about what you're doing. Offer to show people your work in process. An open attitude and positive demeanor will confuse some, put off others, and serve to encourage a few to learn right along with you.

Construction of a big-picture map in the detail described here is a long-term project. Don't feel that you need to complete yours in a week, a month, or even six months. Sketch out the major elements quickly, and fill in detail as you can. You may add bits of new information as you encounter them, or you may summarize your insights at the end of each week. One professional I know developed the habit of recording his observations on management at the end of each day before he turned his computer off. Whatever system you settle on, recognize that thinking in big-picture terms in itself will differentiate you from many of your coworkers.

You Are Here

OK, map's done. Now go back to the place on the chart where you started. Find your desk. See how many lines connect it to others both internally and externally. Are those good lines or nasty lines? Trace the connections forward from your specific contacts to other areas. Are you surprised at how your interactions weave themselves through your firm? Didn't know you were so "integrated," did you? See if you can find clues for smoothing out rough spots and making your interactions even more effective than they are now.

If you find that you personally don't have many interactions with others, check out your group's connections. Generally speaking, the more connected you are, the greater your value to the organization. The reverse is also true. The less integrated you are, the less likely you are to be known or appreciated.

Study the huge panorama of capabilities you've drawn, and use your big-picture map to decide where you want to be in your career and what you'd like to be doing. The information you recorded about the various pieces and the colors you gave them (literally and through descriptions of the people and events within them) provide insight into what you'll need to do to continue to grow and advance.

In the event that you decide to leave your firm for a better opportunity, you'll have an outstanding reference source to formulate questions to ask any potential new employer.

As a fertile starting place for the cultivation of a strong and healthy backbone, the creation of a big-picture map gives you several distinct advantages:

1. It helps protect against the formation of myopic or parochial viewpoints. When you recognize the number and variety of other pieces, you can't help but be more sensitive to the fact that your personal viewpoint is only one of many. With an expanded appreciation for your organization's size and scope, your ideas and comments will reflect your broader understanding and will carry greater weight in any conversation about the business.

2. A big-picture map helps make you more sensitive to and compassionate of other perspectives. This frequently looks like wisdom. Even better, when controversies arise, the big picture helps you see other angles and decide whether or not to engage in battle.

3. Creating a big-picture map helps you throw open the windows and reveal what's going on in the world outside your organization. The big picture can alert you to potential external opportunities and dangers and enable you to manage them before they become urgent. Or before it's too late. *Witch Doctors* authors Micklethwait and Wooldridge underscore the importance of a big-picture focus, noting, "Without some degree of strategic thought or vision, reengineering always risks building a superb machine whose only purpose is to churn out antiquated products."

4. You can use your big-picture map to track the movement of people throughout your organization. You can see who gets promoted and whether promotions tend to happen across functions or in more of a straight-line manner within certain groups. From this, you can determine what you need to do to earn your own advances.

5. Your big-picture map can show special relationships with external groups. Frequency of contact between your organization and another group holds clues to how your company influences and is influenced by others.

The potential benefits of creating a big-picture map are as unique to you as your aspirations. Take as much time as you need in the construction process. See it as an ongoing learning experience, and use it to study your company and your business. You'll be actively enhancing your competence, which you know will build your confidence. Ultimately, with big-picture savvy, you'll be able to take intelligent risks on behalf of your career and your organization.

BACKBONE-BUILDING EXERCISES

• *For Competence*

Draw a big-picture map. Get a pen or pencil, markers or crayons, and get busy.

Right now, before you document your environment, the elements of the picture swirl around in your head, changing places and morphing into confusing new shapes. And you wonder why you get so many headaches?

People move, titles change, companies get bought and sold. Without someplace to "map" these occurrences, a jumbled intellectual mess is inevitable. When you're uncertain of the lay of the land, you hold yourself back from discussions, debates, and decision making.

Take your time. If you feel comfortable, hang your map on your office wall as a work in progress. If this isn't your style, tuck it into your desk drawer.

• *For Confidence*

Study your map. It's the anatomy of your company and industry. Think about it during your coffee break, or when you're taking a head-clearing walk. As you do, you'll become more comfortable with how components fit and how they work. This instills confidence. Micklethwait and Wooldridge, the *Witch Doctors* guys, point out that "computers . . . are often less successful at connecting the strategists in the boardroom to operational staff than managers with long experience with the organization." Even if your experience isn't long, it can be intense. Study.

Create theories, and test them. If you detect routine tension between groups or individuals, for example, locate them on your big-picture map. En route home from work, postulate reasons for the tension. Is a combative manager causing trouble? Inadequate resources? Faulty communication? Inaccurate information going from one group to the other? These and many other variables can create tension.

Watch and listen for information to either substantiate or disprove your theories. Find someone with whom to talk things over. When your theories prove correct, you gain confidence along with useful information. When they're wrong, you still gain insight along with useful information.

• *For Risk Taking*

Working with information from your big-picture map and your independent theory testing, start taking little risks.

Share your map with a trusted friend. Consider going public with it at a team meeting. Ask a question that you wouldn't have dared pose before. Suggest a minor change in operations. Voice an opinion. Talk to someone you've been reluctant to approach.

Keep notes of how others react, and add your observations to your big-picture map. Greater knowledge builds confidence, which enables purposeful and intelligent risk taking.

2

Turn Meetings into Discovery Sessions

AH, MEETINGS. The reality of work that everyone loves to hate and most people complain about until they're sick of their own whining. If only meetings could be done away with, everyone would be so much more productive.

Come on now. You know meetings are important, especially in our team-based businesses today. You know you get more out of some meetings than you ever could just by reading a report. And you know that meetings give you the opportunity to look good in front of people who matter. There are lots of legitimate reasons for having meetings. The problem is that these reasons tend to get lost as we scurry from one meeting to the next.

> **Excellence is to do a common thing in an uncommon way.**
>
> BOOKER T. WASHINGTON

Let's look at a typical weekly lineup to see what happens.

It's Monday morning. You've just arrived at work, and already you're due in a meeting. You grab a notebook and a cup of coffee and head down the hallway to your first meeting of the week. It's a staff meeting, and it happens every Monday morning whether it needs to or not.

What happens in your staff meeting? You hear about last week's doings involving your department. You talk about any company policies that may come into play this week. You review work in process and hear updates from your fellow department staffers. You may talk about a new hire soon to be part of your group. (Rarely do you talk about the newly departed.

You wonder a little about this, but you shrug it off. That's just the way things work here.)

Monday-morning staff meetings always take an hour. Most times, they could be finished in ten minutes, so someone fills the allotted time with a complaint or a problem. This makes everyone else uncomfortable and impatient to get to their "real" work, and by the time the meeting ends, most staffers are crabby. No wonder people hate Monday mornings!

Tuesday is team meeting day. Team meetings are held to share client conversations and requests, to check progress on promises made to the client, to peek at profitability targets, and to investigate the competitive advantage that creativity gives us as we serve our clients. Go, team!

On Wednesday, we meet to talk about synergies between sales and production. These meetings are always testy. Someone invariably misunderstands something, and the loser is the client who doesn't get what was promised on the date specified. Production complains that salespeople promise the moon when the best they could deliver is a piece of clay. Salespeople get impatient with the negative attitudes of production people and hold that even outrageous demands must be met because, after all, "If we don't give clients what they want, someone else will."

On Thursday, we listen to presentations by potential new suppliers. These range from high-tech, big-wow companies to the newest consultant hawking team-building services. These meetings are usually fun, but rarely are the new companies added to our current stable of preferred suppliers. Nobody seems to know how to incorporate them.

On Friday, we meet informally in an ad hoc attempt to gauge our performance over the past week. Where did the time go?

Meetings chew up enormous chunks of time. But they're necessary! And if we examine our frustration with them a little more closely, we'll find that it exists largely because we lack the backbone to change the dynamics of our meetings or to recognize the opportunities for business mastery that each one offers.

Why We Hate Meetings

It's popular to hate meetings. Heaven knows there are lots of reasons why, and here are some of the most common:

- We never know what to expect at this meeting.
- Little meaningful information is shared. Meetings are simply bully pulpits for the organization's speech makers.
- They're too long and unproductive.
- There's no agenda, so the meeting wanders aimlessly from point to point.
- People in the room have a bad attitude toward the project or each other.
- The meeting has no discernible expected outcome.
- Once the meeting is done, nobody is sure what happened, what should happen next, by when it should happen, or who will make it happen.

People with backbone don't waste time hating meetings. They'll tell you that each of these complaints has a solution. Require agendas. Set time limits for individual speakers. Fix bad attitudes, or change the players. State an objective for each meeting, and specify how you expect to accomplish it. Summarize each meeting. Recap what happened and who is expected to do what, by when. Explain resources—where to find them, how to access them, and how to maximize them. Each of these solutions declares the presence of real backbone.

Imagine what would happen at your company if even one of the solutions listed here were actually implemented. Not just once, but once and for all. Wouldn't meetings become far more interesting and productive?

But who, you might ask, would dare impose an agenda where there's never been one before? Who would dare shut down resident windbags? Who would dare call someone on a bad attitude?

And so on, down the list.

We don't dare to exhibit backbone in many of our meetings because—get ready for the rationalizations—we don't want to be rude. We don't want to insult anyone or hurt anyone's feelings. We don't want to overstep our bounds. We don't want to appear judgmental. Or superior. Or condescending. We don't want to sound like a bureaucrat, and we certainly don't want to be politically incorrect.

Instead we are rude, judgmental, and insulting outside the larger meeting group. I've been amazed to hear executives rake each other over the coals of disgust and trash one another's credibility. In private, of course.

The more timid tend to keep their opinions to themselves, but they also don't intervene when someone else is being grilled.

These dysfunctional dynamics describe the worst of what happens when backbone is lacking. If it weren't so sad, so prevalent, and so pervasive, it might be humorous. But it's not. And to the extent that we lack the willingness or ability to cultivate strong backbones and change these meeting problems, our companies will continue to suffer lost productivity, eroded morale, and squandered opportunity.

Is this reason enough to change? Absolutely. Will change happen quickly or easily? Of course not. But it is time to start.

And the fix, believe it or not, is simple. Developing backbone to stick to the point of a business meeting is all that's required. Read the list of complaints again. There's one fundamental reason why people hate meetings: Meetings frequently don't deal with business matters in a way that is credible or satisfying to most of us.

What most of us want to know when we step into a meeting is: What's the point? We get frustrated when there is no apparent answer to this question, and we resent spending time on something that has no discernible purpose. This frustration comes out in personal attacks on those who call such meetings or try, glibly, to talk their way through them.

This looks like a fairly straightforward problem with a ready solution. Why, then, do so many of us continue to waste time and energy in poorly run meetings when we could be doing something more productive? Habit. Inertia. Fear of rocking the boat. Pick a reason; there are many. But looking at it straight on, there are no excuses.

Ok, you say. You would love to take a stand on some of these meeting issues, but you don't feel strong enough at the moment to risk doing so. And if you suddenly stopped going to routine meetings, your nonattendance might be misinterpreted to your disadvantage. For now, you may judge that it's best to continue along as you have in the past.

Fair enough. After all, this book was written to help you take purposeful steps toward the development of backbone, not take a flying leap into the wild, risk-riddled world of the unknown.

How, then, can you begin to get a handle on the meetings you attend, to get more value out of each of them, and to build a bit of backbone with each one?

Read on.

An Everyday Guide to Discovery

Imagine walking into meetings from now on with a sense of anticipation and a desire for new learning. Imagine challenging yourself to describe something at meeting's end that you didn't know before you walked into the room. Wouldn't it be fun to listen in new ways? To view speakers and materials with a new intent? To tease meaning out of a previously mind-numbing ritual?

What other venue brings people together from all levels of your organization and gives you the chance to see, hear, and learn from every one of them, sages and fools alike? The fact of meetings is not going to change, but your approach to them can. Starting right now, I invite you to envision every meeting as a discovery session for advanced business learning. Listen up. Pay attention. An awful lot happens that isn't on any agenda.

Business/Industry

Want to know how captains of industry get to be captains? They dig into the business and fill their blood full of its drama and excitement. They watch how events take shape, who influences the course, and where money comes from to create new tomorrows. They live the business! These people are *intense*!

But back to your meeting blues . . .

At your next meeting, wake up your mind. Think in broader terms about the work you do for the company that hired you. Instead of dropping into a catatonic state when the drone of the firm starts up, listen for information about customers, suppliers, competitors, pricing, distribution, whatever. Tie it to what you do. Think about how your work influences (or could influence) the other developments you hear about.

Try to understand what your products and services mean to the ongoing success of your customers. What do they do with your stuff? How do they handle it? When you mess up, what happens on their end?

Listen for talk about your competitors. Think about ways you can help your company gain or maintain an advantage. (Remember, before you can determine an advantage, you have to understand the game.) That power outage last week shut down your competitor's production line for three full days: did you make hay?

People with backbone pay attention to all this industry information. They gather company intelligence and think hard about how to capitalize on it.

Look around the room. Who's here? These are your partners in competition. What are they good at? Why are those attributes germane to your business? What do you and your associates create within your company that isn't available anywhere else?

When you start thinking like this and paying attention to what's being said, you'll probably get a lot more excited about the business propositions available to your company. Are you going to do this at every meeting? Of course not. But try it at the next one and see if it changes your perspective.

Chemistry (Human Relations)

Chemistry is a classic arena for fascinating discovery. Think about chemistry in a traditional sense, how people mix materials together with a specific result in mind. How come so many experiments blow up? Remember those spectacular concoctions in high school that smelled like something you couldn't describe and smoked and foamed in ways that were truly awesome? I remember a kid creating an active volcano for a science fair—the kind you made with flour and water and filled with sulfur and something else. When it started to erupt, it made people chuckle and ooh and ahh. But when it kept flowing all over the tabletop and then onto the floor, the humor disappeared in a hurry.

The same kinds of unpredictable things happen with people. Interpersonal chemistry can produce fluke reactions. Check it out at your next meeting. See who's being mixed together in the room and with what intended result. Observe body language. Listen to voice quality, and notice fidgeting and posturing. Note who sits where, how close a person is to some and how distant from others. Watch how the conversation baton gets passed around the room, who fumbles the pass and who accepts it smoothly and with grace. Listen for abrupt halts to the conversation, and watch for reactions when this happens. Notice who smiles, who frowns, and who appears to be catatonic. People with backbone pay attention to this stuff and use their knowledge of individuals' chemistry to assemble their own productive meetings.

You can watch different colleagues at different meetings or, if you prefer, monitor the same person over several meetings to see how he or she interacts with a wide range of others. For fun, you can mentally design your own periodic table of human behavior elements and classify your colleagues by how they react in proximity to others. Watch out, though. This can become so involving that you lose track of the purpose of your meeting!

Here's an example of chemistry in action. Marlene is a senior executive at a bank. She's a caustic old woman who's been around for twenty-plus years, and right now she's suspicious about what a bunch of quality-improvement volunteers are doing. (Detect the acid?) The volunteers, employees from several departments within the company, are looking for ways to improve customer satisfaction in two areas of the firm's operations. They happened to be poking around in processes that fall under her control, and she didn't like it. She was incensed at the questions already raised by their work, and she complained bitterly to the head of human resources. She could hardly believe that the company was "letting the clowns run the circus." (Oh, my. Is this empowerment?)

When she learned that the president had initiated the project—and in fact encouraged the "clowns" in this work—she decided to see firsthand what they were up to. Leveraging her position, she concocted a reason to address one of the groups and arranged to make a presentation at their next meeting.

On the appointed day, Marlene arrives early and arranges herself at the head of the table. As lower-ranking employees enter the room, she greets each with a tight smile and a curt nod. The chemistry is churlish. You can almost see a swirling, smoky brew being created.

When all are assembled, Marlene delivers a clipped and superficial speech about the value of customer satisfaction. She warns members that their job is to find more reasons to say yes to customers than to say no (see index finger punching air for effect) and that they especially need to be fiscally responsible in their work. (That triggers the eyeball glaze.) She says they especially need to be mindful of the time they are spending in these meetings (as she studies the ceiling), and of the cost to the organization when they are away from their "real" jobs.

She then magnanimously offers her support. Questions?

As Marlene sweeps from the room, shoulders slump and heavy sighs explode. The terseness of Marlene's presentation has withered the group. Even the most enthusiastic members are now tense and unsure about their work. What, precisely, are they supposed to do with the information and "support" offered by this cretin? The words had been positive, but the delivery meant what? To invoke Emerson: "What you are speaks so loudly that I can't hear what you say."

On that particular day, Marlene opened a toxic vial of poison and poured it over the work of these impressionable employees. She was subtle but effective. When the president learned of the incident, he shrugged and said, "Oh, that's just the way she is. She won't harm anyone."

She did harm the effort. Two volunteers quit, and the rest finished the project carefully. No revelations came from the work, so guess what? It was considered a nice experiment but probably a waste of time. How many other innovations will this firm endorse?

It's hard to overstate the power of human relations chemistry, even when it occurs subtly. When bad chemistry yields unproductive situations, savvy people try to understand the elements in the mix and why the brew went bad.

The Wonder of Words

In every meeting you attend, you'll hear rich and varied vocabulary. Some meetings crackle with locutions that describe the politics of a situation. Some buzz along on technical terms. Some sizzle with sophisticated jargon; others ramble along more pedestrian platitudes. It's all backbone-building material because it builds competence.

Listen to how sentences are cast. There are speakers who love to use rhetorical questions. Some like to mix short declarative sentences with longer, more reflective ones. Others drone on in paragraphs laden with big, heavy words. (They're very serious, these people.) Notice how your energy level fluctuates with different speakers. Can you relate it to the way a speaker uses language?

Notice how people react to certain words—some are loaded with meaning that differs from the speaker's intent. From time to time, you'll hear people complain that "we're arguing over semantics." Yes! Semantics has to do with the meaning of words. If I say, as one of my clients did, that I need big people to get a job done, I may or may not be alluding to physical size. (My client wasn't, but one gentleman in the room didn't realize this and stepped up to the challenge. He was painfully embarrassed when others snickered.) Pay attention to what happens when certain words are used.

Business buzzwords create ambiguity. If they mean anything at all, they usually don't mean the same thing to everyone subjected to them at a given time. *Empowerment*, for example, means what? To managers, it means giving staffers the keys to expanded decision making. That's a little scary to some folks. To staffers, *empowerment* means a bunch of management yada-yada usually followed by criticism of some sort.

Mental pictures appear automatically in response to a word, and these pictures differ. Shared understanding is rare. Yet, you assume that when you use a word, others automatically know what you mean. People with backbone clarify. They paint word pictures so their audiences don't have to conjure up their own. They know how easily people can get tangled up in energy-wasting misunderstandings.

Take this group of executives, for example, who were debating the necessity of adding a new position to the company's leadership ranks. Everyone used the same term to describe the function of the position— operations—but few had the same kind of position in mind. One guy felt the role should be an internal systems architect and personnel disciplinarian. Another guy felt the role should cover a broader range of authority and include interactions with clients and partners. Hold on; someone else objected to this positioning, feeling that his authority with corporate salespeople would be usurped. Still another guy felt that the job should be limited to implementing decisions made by them (the management group). The last guy argued for the inclusion of this new role at the highest strategic levels of the organization.

These guys were using the same word (operations) and growing frustrated because they all had different mental pictures of what that word described. They began to distrust each other's motivations, and pretty soon rumblings

> **Mastery is not something that strikes in an instant, like a thunderbolt, but a gathering power that moves steadily through time, like weather.**
>
> JOHN GARDNER

of political intrigue surfaced. When they tried using different descriptors, a realization dawned on them. The source of their confusion was that silly word. Operations. When they set it aside and began describing more specifically what they wanted the role to accomplish for the firm, they were able to elevate their discourse to more productive levels.

Command of language is a backbone enhancer. When you can describe precisely what's in your head so that people can see what you see, the power surge from being understood is electrifying. Also, be aware that some people use words with a specific intent to confuse. People with backbone don't let that happen.

Foreign Language (Terms, Body Language)

Get careful with words. Then remind yourself that actions speak louder. (This backbone-building stuff will challenge you.) Your objective with this observational mind-set is to monitor strangeness in both language and behavior. If there's a term you don't understand, note it. Note unfamiliar phrases or usages in a context that doesn't make sense to you. As you gain backbone, you'll start asking for explanations the moment you hear puzzling constructions, but in the meantime, record them for further reflection.

The discovery of "foreign language" extends beyond mere words. How people arrange themselves in a room may be unfamiliar to you. How certain associates address others may be different. Younger workers may follow behavior protocols that depart from traditional norms.

Think about why you prefer your own company's offices as the site for potentially contentious or impactful negotiation meetings. Familiar surroundings put you at ease and require others to adapt to your customs. Something as ordinary as a favorite restaurant gives you an advantage because you know the people, the protocol, and the menu. Fewer distractions and decisions mean more available energy and attention for the matters to be resolved. Backbone-savvy folks know and use this principle.

Here's a case in point. A number of years ago, I traveled with several associates to the headquarters of a business partner in another state. This partner had failed dismally in the delivery of services that were critical to our own performance on a multimillion-dollar project, and the purpose of our meeting was to pull the business. Naturally, the partner wanted to host the meeting (home field advantage), and from a practical standpoint—all relevant materials were kept at his location—it made sense. More important, the partner knew that by having us on his turf, he had a negotiating edge.

We arrived at the airport in plenty of time to drive to the company's headquarters, but we got lost along the way. (The guy suspected we would—his offices were out in the boonies.) By the time we regained our bearings, we were thirty minutes late to the appointment. Of course, our tardiness was used in a raised-eyebrow fashion to subtly question our competence. Other disruptions caused by their workaday routines (breaks, workers paged for phone calls, lunch delivered during a tense interchange) made our job more difficult and unnerving. The comfort advantage was definitely theirs, and we were forced to work harder to maintain our agenda amid myriad distractions. Luckily, with backbones firmly engaged, we were able to do so, and our mission was accomplished by day's end.

As you settle into your next meeting, pay attention to elements that are foreign to you or that you've missed in the past. You'll gain insight into how others operate, and you'll build a reservoir of knowledge that will serve you well in future situations.

By becoming an astute observer, you'll gain access to secrets that less attentive workers never learn. Your confidence in managing a variety of situations will be enhanced, and you may find that your backbone has become not only more visible but also more reliable.

Culture Club

Foreignness looked at a little differently is diversity. All those meetings you attend overflow with live examples of culture and diversity, as well as generation and gender components.

Corporate culture and diversity are two of the hottest topics in business. Many people struggle to understand what they're all about. Edgar Schein, a noted organizational culture expert, says that any group with a stable membership and a history of shared learning will have developed some level of culture. The keys are stability of membership and shared learning. According to Schein, groups experiencing high rates of member turnover don't have a chance to develop culture. And groups led by people who haven't had to deal with challenging events don't have the opportunity to develop shared assumptions.

What's the culture like where you work? What assumptions do you and your coworkers share? You'll discover them as you listen to meeting discussions. If turnover has been high, as is the case in many organizations, you can expect some frustration as people try to understand one another and the tasks at hand.

Complicating the development of shared assumptions is diversity. Different strokes for different folks is a lovely premise for life, but in an organizational setting, it creates more than a little confusion. Whose way is the right way in a given situation? Whose perspective is most accurate?

And what's all this got to do with backbone? Understanding, folks. Developing the competence to intuit culture and know how it affects performance is a backbone builder. Think about it. When are you most likely to stand up or speak out: when you know what's going on, or when you're dazed and confused?

Along these lines, remember that age and gender color many interactions too. Wisdom and experience, once highly prized qualities, have been redefined by some employers as calcified thinking and staidness. Youth is now hailed in many quarters for its energy and fearlessness in the face of experimentation and change. Tension is inevitable. Misunderstandings abound.

The same is true for differences between the sexes. Here, particularly, the need for backbone is critical. Watch what happens when issues carry high emotional content. Some people keep quiet until they can't stand it anymore, and then they explode, often in ways that are not beneficial to them. Others refuse to comment at all. When a power imbalance exists, true resolution of a problem is rare.

Sensitivity to cultural differences is required training because people will sometimes use these differences to confuse and distract. Or worse, as excuses for why they didn't get something done. A healthy backbone will help you counter such nonsense.

Presentation Technology

From laser pointers to laptop cinematography, the world of presentations has become incredibly complex and creative. But have presentations become more effective? As you observe multimedia extravaganzas, turn your attention to how the medium influences the message. Are you wowed by the technic and distracted from the meaning? If so, the tool may be suspect. Does the equipment behave temperamentally? This is not the way to convey a coherent and powerful message!

The combination of younger workers and agile technologies gives many presentations an MTV-like feel—lots of color, sound, and fast-moving graphics. When the audience is attuned to this style (and more of them are, according to worker demographics), the result may be powerful. But keep this question in mind as you experience your next high-tech meeting: What is the purpose of this show? Using a fantastic tool because it is available is not necessarily the wisest choice.

The best presentations engage us in the content by capturing our attention and demonstrating concepts through pictures and color as well as with imaginative words. This is important information!

But in a society that demands entertainment in exchange for our time, too many of us have become passive observers. We love whizbang, but we forget sometimes to ask what it was all about. The entertainment capabilities of our business tools may foster this trend. Stand firm, backbone people. Study presentations instead of being idly amused by them. You'll gain practical information for evaluating and selecting the proper tools to make your own presentations powerful and memorable. Then, select 'em and use 'em. You know by now that people with backbone don't follow the crowd. They advance with a purpose in mind.

Physics

When you attend business meetings with a physics perspective, you consciously study the sources and uses of power. Think about matter and energy during meetings. Be aware of acoustics and how volume affects pace. Observe the transference of heat and how people will scramble to get away from it. Watch how magnetism and radiation influence results.

Imagine how interesting it would be to track the flow of energy through your workplace. Where does it start? What stops it cold? When energy disappears from one setting, where does it go? (Hint: When enthusiasm turns to apathy, you can be assured the energy is still there somewhere. Chances are it will surface in a surprising way later.) Note agreement and disagreement around a conference room. Who's lining up where? Why? What patterns are here?

Thinking in physics terms makes managing conflict a little more entertaining and a whole lot easier. The next time Jack takes off on Barry, imagine it's an example of atomic fission happening right at work. Watch those sparks fly! And look at Barry's charred expression. It never fails to let everyone know the outcome. See how much more relaxed you are? And now you know: There is life after the bomb.

I was involved in a strategic planning session once with fourteen other people. Lots of important themes were raised, but the discussion meandered in a squishy sort of way. It was pretty evident that few people in the room felt equipped or empowered to make any direct remarks about what the company was currently doing or what the future should look like. You could tell they were afraid of something, but you couldn't put your finger on what it was.

After several hours of this noncommittal dancing, the CEO lost his temper. "Who in the hell is going to say something that makes sense here? None of you people can tell me what you think. None of you people seems to know what's going on out there. Why are we wasting this time? Is this the best we can do? What the hell are we paying you people for?"

Bodies squirmed. Heads bowed. Eyes were averted. An uncomfortable silence engulfed the room. No one knew what to do next. I was intrigued by this paralysis of the company's most senior executives, and as I scanned the room, I caught the eye of the CEO. I was amazed to see a twinkle. A second later, he gave me a conspiratorial wink. He knew exactly what he was doing, and it was clear that at that moment, he was enjoying himself immensely. He was looking for someone with backbone to take a stand on something. Anything.

He ordered a short break and said he hoped to God someone would have something intelligent to contribute when we came back.

During the break, a small group of guys had their heads together over in a corner. They were comparing notes, and you could tell they were negotiating something. A coin flew high and fell with a muffled thud. One of the guys sighed.

After the break, the guy who sighed stood up and said, "The new internal system we've been talking about is the wrong one for us." A few quick gasps punctuated an otherwise stone-cold silence.

The CEO replied, "Tell me why."

It was a meeting changer.

After a few hesitant remarks, the sigh-guy hit his stride, and he grew stronger with every reason he gave. The meeting took off. It was a lot more contentious than it had been and a lot more productive, too. How powerful a little backbone can be.

Hold on, you say. He spoke up out of fear, not backbone. That group of guys who gathered at the break figured participation was a requirement for saving their jobs. Maybe. But sometimes you need a jolt of fear to get serious about building backbone. Now that the sigh-guy has successfully launched a controversial opinion, he'll be less hesitant in the future. So will the people who jumped into the discussion and lived to tell about it.

Understanding the sources and uses of power has tremendous implications for your career. Having the backbone to leverage these sources and uses will set you apart from those who shy away from or remain oblivious to them.

Schedule Your Attendance

See how much you can learn at meetings? It's remarkable how much smarter you can get when you tune your mind differently. But I know that, even with this wealth of knowledge at your disposal, you'll still sometimes wish you could skip a meeting or two. Maybe even strike an entire day's worth to focus attention on a project you've been putting off. So, do it. You'll have to engage your backbone, of course, but here's how.

Take out your calendar of meetings for tomorrow, and list why your attendance is important. Now ask yourself some questions: If you attend a meeting purely to obtain information, could you get the information another way? If you attend a meeting to be updated on a variety of projects, but only a select few are relevant to you, could you limit your time in the meeting or get updates some other way? If you have information to distribute, can you do so without requiring people to assemble?

If your meetings are routine, must you attend every one? If a meeting includes most of your colleagues, could someone brief you on it later?

Be realistic in answering these questions, and get serious about how you use your time. Bolting from meetings because they bore you to death is not a good reason to skip them. (And besides, you won't be bored anymore now that you have all kinds of interesting things to watch for.)

One Question You Should Always Ask

Anytime you walk into a meeting, get into the habit of asking this question: "What are we doing today?" If an agenda has been prepared, you'll get it. If no agenda exists, persist with your question until someone (preferably the meeting's host) answers it.

Remember that the primary reason for frustration and irritation with meetings is that so few are conducted to satisfy a particular objective.

When a group gathers—in a weekly team meeting, for example—make sure there is a specific purpose. If the purpose is to update everyone on the progress of a project, do so. If it is to discuss and resolve a problem or proposition, stick with the substance and avoid distractions. If other issues surface in midcourse, note them and set a time and place to address them.

Asking, "What are we doing today?" sounds like a commonsense technique, but few people practice it. Why? Because the culture in many companies allows people to free-form their way through meetings. Casual chatter before a meeting starts is encouraged in the name of bonding and team building. Getting everyone's opinions on a topic feels like empowerment and sharing. These are positives, but only when they're managed.

If you don't get an answer to your simple question, quietly and politely excuse yourself. Eventually, people will understand that the time and energy invested in meetings come at a cost to the organization, to the project, and to each other.

BACKBONE-BUILDING EXERCISES

• *For Competence*

Tune your brain and fix your attention during a meeting. Will you study chemistry today or business? Will you track the movement of power in a physics-like way?

Write down what you see and hear. Play with it from different angles. Internal chemistry sets off physics-like chain reactions. That influences the business by igniting spirited debates that generate new ideas.

• *For Confidence*

Before meetings begin, try to predict how the session will progress, where it will hit snags, who will redirect it, and what outcomes are likely. Compare your predictions with actual events, and keep track of your successes.

When you leave a meeting, try to think of two things you know now that you didn't before the meeting started. Multiply that by the number of meetings you'll attend today, and appreciate how much smarter you'll be on the way home tonight.

- ### *For Risk Taking*
Ask, "What are we doing today?" If you're satisfied with the answer, stay put. If you're not satisfied with the answer, excuse yourself. Your action will speak louder than any protestation you can make against wasted time, sloppy thinking, and misdirected effort.

Quit complaining about wasteful meetings. If they're worthless, don't go.

Become a Jotter

Now THAT MEETINGS are enticing you with broad new vistas of knowledge, you'll want to make note of some things. But in many firms, it's considered a little amateurish to take personal notes. Sometimes it's even considered gauche. You see, we live in an age of studied sophistication—almost nonchalance—about what's going on right in front of us. (A lot of people who were too cool to take notes in school still are.)

Distributed knowledge, extensive networks, and close-knit teams enable lots of (other) people to provide bits of information while software integrates it into one big whole. By tapping this knowledge electronically, effortlessly, you have everything you need at your fingertips. Theoretically, anyway.

> **There's always something new by looking at the same thing over and over.**
> JOHN UPDIKE

Given this, you might wonder why you'd take your own notes. Why be distracted when someone else has been assigned or when you know you'll receive an electronic recap of the meeting, same day? Why, indeed. Because note taking is a big backbone-supporting activity. For several reasons.

First, if you don't write things down, you're likely to forget. And you know how lame "I forgot" sounds.

Second, your observations and thoughts are unique and important. The assigned note taker in any meeting or conference may or may not know as much about the subjects covered as you do. When you jot things down as they occur—events, comments, your own thoughts on a matter under discussion—you capture the reality of a situation. Otherwise, perception becomes reality, and you know how slippery that slope can be.

Third, by recording what you see and hear, you create a context. This is a benefit because nothing happens in a vacuum. When you capture the surrounding circumstances of an event, you better understand the catalysts. The formal, "official" notes you receive are likely to be condensed; they may even be incomplete. Major chunks of discussion often get lopped off of recaps. With your own notes supplementing the formal ones, summarized decisions will mean more to you because you'll have the context within which they were made.

Fourth, pragmatically speaking, when you disagree with someone who didn't take notes and is working strictly from memory, you'll have the upper hand.

Finally, by taking notes, you engage your brain in what's going on. You improve your posture, literally and figuratively, when you have paper and pen in hand. Instead of sitting zombielike until a meeting's over, you'll dissect who's saying what and why. You'll find this mental engagement refreshing, believe me.

Some people have a bad attitude about note taking in general. CYA (cover your [ahem]) activity, they call it. Nothing more, nothing less. People with backbone don't see things that way at all. In fact, when they meet these bad-attitude types, they ignore them. And they keep on taking competence-building notes.

Sometimes there are nasty consequences when you don't take notes. Danielle, a project manager in a $250 million direct marketing agency, suffered major stress and acute embarrassment because she didn't write something down. Here's what happened. Danielle, in conjunction with a marketing manager, an artist, and several production people, had created a fantastic new direct marketing program for a longtime client. The account was under pressure from this client, who wanted to see innovative ideas and breakthrough creative. In search of these, the client was inviting submissions from competing firms. (They'll turn on you like that sometimes.)

Danielle was responsible for pulling together all relevant details of the proposal, including pricing, from an assortment of external partners. The proposal was exceptional, and the client was thrilled, especially with the budget. As presented, the budget for this exciting new program was a full

30 percent lower than the nearest competitor, despite the sophisticated communications and tracking technologies it employed. Suspecting an error somewhere, the client asked for a careful review by Danielle and her team.

They scrutinized the program and the numbers. Satisfied and comfortable, they assured the client that all was in order.

The deal was signed, a purchase order was cut, and work began. Within two months, the project was over budget. Distressed, Danielle began investigating. One supplier was billing her at a rate of 23 cents per record when her recollection was that the supplier had quoted 18 cents per record. (More than a million and a half records were involved in the project.) Checking the proposal numbers, she found that indeed she had built 18 cents per record into the budget. Before getting on the phone with the supplier, she reviewed her file, looking for confirmation of the 18 cents per record quotation. There was none.

The telephone conversation was tense. Both Danielle and her contact at the supplier had a great deal at stake with this job. Their reputations notwithstanding, big bucks were on the line. Danielle played the friendship and loyalty cards—she and her contact had spent long hours together over the years and had done great work. She needed help here and sorely hoped that her friend and colleague could provide it. After a moment's hesitation, the supplier said, "So sorry." His firm had just announced efforts internally to tighten the ship; profits had slipped over the past quarter. Any wiggle room that might have existed while the proposal was being drafted was long gone.

> Take note of that; his Lordship says he will turn it over in what he is pleased to call his mind.
>
> LORD WESTBURY, BARRISTER (1800–1873)

He referred to his pricing guideline for the program. Not finding record of any oral quote (naturally), he said the standard fee with the full volume discount allowable was 23 cents per record. He would not have been authorized to reduce it by nearly 30 percent to give the discounted rate of 18 cents per record, he explained. And though he was truly sympathetic to her predicament, without written proof, there was little he could do for her.

In the rush of putting together a multimillion-dollar project with intense competition and impossible deadlines, a missing note regarding an oral quotation from a trusted and longtime supplier may seem insignificant. It isn't.

The program, though successful, did not meet the frothy expectations of a jazzed-up client. Furthermore, the simple per-record error eroded the program's margin to a disappointingly low level. Danielle was fortunate to have a healthy backbone. Though she fervently wished she could undo her mistake and produce some proof in her favor, she couldn't. She decided to bite the bullet, confess her error, and take whatever consequences came her way.

Will she ever forget the lesson? It's unlikely. Did she deserve to be fired for making such a costly mistake on such a huge account at such a crucial competitive moment? Some would say yes. But replacing her would have created additional expense in time and experience lost. And no one new ever comes with a mistake-free guarantee.

OK, so taking notes during meetings—even small ones between you and one or two other people—is important. What about using notes to sort out your thoughts on a project? That works well too. Let's say you're uncertain about what to include in a report. You have disparate bits of data. You have pressure from conflicting camps about what the report should say. You don't feel strongly about the report one way or another—in fact, your greatest concern is getting the darn thing done.

By making notes about the report, the people who will receive it, and the major facts involved, you can create a concise, intelligent document aimed at the ones who want it. Observe.

> **He listens well who takes notes.**
>
> DANTE

Barbara, Gary, Robert, and Lew are to be on the receiving end of your report. Barbara runs production, Gary is the finance guy, Robert is the procurement specialist, and Lew takes care of shipping. You have all sorts of interesting information on new materials, offshore suppliers, price haggling, and so forth. But what all four want to know is when materials will be in, how long production will take, how much the client will be billed, and how soon finished goods will ship. That's a pretty concise outline for a report.

Arrange your notes accordingly. Save extended explanations and stories of heroic negotiations for coffee breaks or for the recipient who asks for them.

People with backbone don't lace reports with streams of interesting but at-the-moment irrelevant findings. They respect the need for quick and accurate news. They don't worry about being too brief and therefore not getting credit for being as smart as they really are. They don't worry that without complete background information, their report may be misinterpreted or misunderstood. They give the facts formally and stand prepared to elaborate from their notes as the need arises.

Study Your Notes

Now, then. You're happy that you've got good notes, even great ones. Excellent. Read 'em. Think about 'em. I've seen many professionals take copious notes during meetings and conferences and then file them away, never to be looked at again. Having done the same myself at more conferences than I care to think about, I recognize that there is some learning to be had from the process of making notes, as discussed in the beginning of this chapter. When auditory, intellectual, and motor skills combine, learning goes deeper and lasts longer, say the experts. But the real education comes when you reflect upon your notes and apply them to everyday situations.

When you can revisit what you wrote, apply it to a business situation, and take action based on this, you'll appreciate the power of note taking. A full set of notes was the clincher in the following high-stakes situation.

Jim, the chief operating officer of a large and successful family-owned firm, was contemplating the termination of a top-level manager, Roy. Roy is a family member who has worked in the business for five years. Prior to this, Roy had worked in other nonrelated and noncompeting businesses. Jim had recently been hired from outside the firm and given wide responsibility and authority with strong support from both the family and the board of directors. Roy's attitude toward Jim was cavalier, even contemptuous. It had been from day one.

Roy resented Jim. He wasn't a family member, and his background didn't specifically match their industry. Furthermore, Jim had dared to try to hold Roy—a family member!—accountable for results in his area of the company. Jim was always asking questions about what Roy was doing and what he was accomplishing. Nobody else had ever challenged him like that, not even his brothers. Where did Jim get off pushing him so hard?

The rap on Roy was that he had traveled far and wide working on special projects over the past couple of years and had returned very little of value to the firm. He gave only superficial reports of his travels. He didn't follow up on promising sales situations. He refused to be held accountable for his time or his travels. And he badmouthed Jim.

Because he was a family member with responsibility for a substantial area of the company, his actions were highly visible and influential. The messages he was sending and the behavior he was subtly promoting were all wrong. In Jim's mind, Roy was clearly flaunting his family status to the long-term detriment of the company. He also believed it had reached a level of seriousness that justified moving Roy out.

The situation created enormous tension and quickly became the subject of many high-level discussions. Terminating Roy would create major conflict with some family members who were sympathetic. (This sympathy was actually personal affection and had nothing to do with Roy's performance in the business.) But anything less at this stage would destroy Jim's credibility and encourage Roy to continue in his ways. There wasn't an option.

Months of discussion passed. Data were gathered and opinions were aired. Jim took copious notes and studied them often, pondering the implications of a range of comments and warnings. He evaluated his own objectivity and what stake he personally had in resolving—or not resolving—this situation. He reflected on Roy's behavior in isolation and as it impacted the work of others. With comprehensive notes and serious study time, Jim decided to go ahead with the termination. He wasn't happy about it, but he knew it was the right solution to a very sticky situation.

Would Jim have had the backbone to fire Roy without his notes? Maybe. He could have just snapped one day and fired him on the spot. But Jim's notes allowed him to describe with accuracy a long-standing problem, its current impact on the business, and the long-term implications of keeping Roy on staff. That's a lot more convincing and effective than "I'd just had it with the guy."

In addition, by carefully noting and studying this complex situation, Jim had all the information he needed to spell out what his expectations were for the next manager. His written notes provided a complete case study and helped him to recruit and indoctrinate the new manager. By his closing the loop on this uncomfortable situation, Jim's standing with the board skyrocketed. Family squabbles intensified for a brief time following Roy's ouster, but they soon subsided as business performance improved.

Backbone pays.

Use Notes to Refine Big-Picture Pieces

In addition to helping you clarify your thinking and make better decisions, the information included in your notes is fodder for your big-picture map. A thorough review of your notes helps establish and confirm big-piece connections and influences. It helps you postulate the ramifications of your decisions inside and outside your firm. It protects against blind spots.

Jim recognized his vulnerability as a new guy and a nonrelative. He made an effort to understand the big-picture pieces that Roy touched. He talked to people inside and outside the firm who had worked with Roy. Even after the termination, he kept his ears open at association meetings for talk of the firm and Roy. His sensitivity to the big picture helped him counteract people who would have loved to cast the situation as a personal battle between Roy and Jim. In those (lazy) kinds of blood-is-thicker-than-water arguments, the organization always ends up the loser.

Jim's broader observations helped him to refine big-picture pieces and also to uncover red flags to watch for in the future. Roy had a few buddies still in-house. 'Nough said.

Comprehensive big-picture information can pump steel into your spine at decisive moments.

Use Notes to Refresh Others' Recollections

Carefully kept notes can also help you refresh the memories of people who conveniently forget how events transpired. Lots of everyday conflict revolves around whose version of a story is correct. With notes, you can re-create discussions, time lines, even outside factors that impacted a situation. You have a context that others don't, and because of this, your story wins.

Throughout the ranks of workers, precious time is routinely wasted in arguing over what are mere recollections. Many business discussions today involve animated exchanges of "fact," and the more intense the debate, the more irrefutable the facts. Without a reference guide (your notes), such talks can—and do—drag on for the long haul, stifling any meaningful activity toward resolution.

People with backbone know that if they're going to debate, they're going to have notes. They use their notes to remind others of what's already been established. If consensus was reached earlier, they remind folks and move on. Where conflict remains, they refer to their notes to re-create discussions and the context within which they were conducted. If new information or different circumstances arise, past impressions and opinions may in fact change, and people with backbone are OK with that. But without notes, they realize that accurate recollection of an original position is nearly impossible. Movement in a different direction, then, becomes hopeful meandering instead of purposeful progress. Fact-finding sessions veer off point, priorities shift frequently, and some problems seem solution-resistant.

People with backbone use notes unashamedly to keep everyone on point and unmuddled.

Highlight Answers; Use 'Em Again

People with backbone also keep track of useful notes and refer to them when they encounter new, but somehow similar, challenges. Steve had recently taken over as sales manager for a fast-growing educational products distributor. His sixteen reps were young, hungry, and full of energy. They pushed him hard in two major areas—order servicing and bonuses. They wanted products shipped fast and accurately, and they wanted bonuses to be based on gross sales, not on delivery less returns, and definitely not on overall margin.

Steve's prior sales management experience had been with traditional insurance products. In that job, Steve's guys were a shade older and a lot more conservative. They were interested in bonuses, too, but the company's formula, once understood, was accepted without much comment or question. As for delivery, they didn't worry much about it. Home office was responsible for getting paperwork to the customer. Once Steve gave these folks the rule book, most of them fell in line pretty well.

Not so for the new reps. They liked to challenge, especially their pay, and they always wanted to negotiate up. They had scores of questions about the formulas used by the company, and they moaned about pokey distribution. They said it made customers mad and cost them repeat business.

Referring to his old binder, Steve borrowed some of the techniques he'd used in managing his most aggressive insurance salespeople. He found that although the situations were markedly different, some of the tips he'd learned then were helpful with his new, more unruly gang. His old notes helped him face the new challenges with a heck of a backbone. The youngsters were impressed.

Am I suggesting that for every job you hold in every company you work for, you should keep reams of notes? Only if you're a pack rat with a big barn in which to store them all. But whenever you make a big decision, negotiate an important consensus, or discover a missing ingredient that leads to success, highlight the information in your notes that helped you get there. Although no two situations are entirely similar, there is surprising consistency in the types of problems that present themselves. Why reinvent the wheel each time you encounter new or rough terrain?

People with strong backbones make notes. They study them, learn from them, and use them to think more carefully and completely. Want to grow a backbone? Become a jotter.

BACKBONE-BUILDING EXERCISES

- *For Competence*

Stock up on notepads, and get into the habit of carrying one everywhere. You'll look seriously professional, and the notepad will remind you to pay attention to what's going on.

Summarize what's happening. Note time, place, people, subject matter, major events, and whatever else feeds in to your discussion or meeting. Doodling, by the way, disqualifies you.

• *For Confidence*

Study your notes. Develop a context for situations that are puzzling or contentious. Pay attention to what people said and what they subsequently did. See if you can figure out what caused any differences.

Save your notes in a form that allows you to refer to them in the future. Don't worry about building that storage barn. A few binders or electronic files should be sufficient to retain your most important lessons.

• *For Risk Taking*

Buck convention; take notes. Who cares if people think you're a rummy? When you've got information, insight, and ammo in a hotly contested spot, who's going to have the last word?

Invite reality checks. Share your notes with a trusted friend, and see if your perspectives match. Listen to different viewpoints with respect for their validity.

With notes in hand, take a stand. You may be wrong sometimes, but that's OK. Acknowledge your mistake and move on. What a backbone you'll be making!

4

Get Eyes Wise

EYES ENABLE VISION.

Think about that. Think beyond the physiology of eyesight to encompass imagination, conception, discernment, and foresight. You've got an awesome tool in that head of yours.

The physiology of sight is pretty impressive in its own right, but your eyes working in conjunction with your brain enable you to do the extraordinary. You can read between the lines. See below the surface. Envision the future. See into the real meaning of what's before you. Picture yourself. Look forward. Form a mental picture. See the light.

Eyes also bring you reality. Life as it unfolds. Events as they happen. There is no emotional coloring to what your eyes take in; that comes only after the brain has gotten involved.

> **The whole secret of the study of nature lies in learning how to use one's eyes.**
> GEORGE SAND

This is an important distinction and one that many people forget. Events can feel so darn upsetting, but your eyes bring you only the actuality of them. When you can learn to truly see what's there without speculating on why or how it got there, you begin to gain powerful perspective. As a friend of mine says so often, "Things are the way they are, and they're going to stay that way until we change them." It's vital to see what is, before you can begin to envision what might be.

This premise has tremendous implications at work. How many times have you heard someone rail against something that happened? The client reneged on an agreement. A manager was caught embezzling company resources. A promising candidate declined your firm's excellent job offer and went, instead, to a competitor. These things happen every single day all around the world. We can see them for what they are and determine our position in that light, or we can refuse to see what's there and attempt to create a different reality. The wise use their eyes to see what's there. They know that true vision comes later. Eyes take in all sorts of cues and clues from the environment, turning them over to your mind and heart for interpretation, discovery, and action.

What Eyes Show You

Stepping to the other side of the eyeball, we know that eyes also show and tell. You can tell when you are the apple of someone's eye; you see it in the special sparkle when the person looks at you. You can tell when people are uncomfortable; they won't look at you. You can discern enthusiasm, humor, fear, anger, boredom, confusion, and all sorts of other emotions just by watching people's eyes.

Said St. Jerome, "The face is the mirror of the mind, and eyes without speaking confess the secrets of the heart."

You can detect when words are insincere by noting the expression in the speaker's eyes. You can likewise sense when someone has emotionally checked out; there are vacancy signs where the eyeballs should be. Then there are those who have played the slot machine of life and lost; their eyes say "tilt."

Eyes show disapproval, too, and anyone who has said or done something that goes against the grain has experienced the pain of "the look."

A brand manager for a major bathroom fixtures company was in the middle of a presentation to the board of directors regarding a new marketing approach that he was taking with his product line. At one point, he justified a radical step by noting the weaknesses of traditional methods. His associates, steeped in those very methods, "turned with a ghastly pang, and cursed him with their eyes." He was visibly taken aback. He started backpedaling almost immediately. And there went his credibility.

Rolling eyeballs have long been recognized as an indicator of frustration, disagreement, or disdain. It's interesting to see how subtly some people can roll their eyes, and how embarrassed they can be when caught.

One executive confessed that in his younger days, he would roll his eyes out of bad habit. When he realized what he had done, he'd cough, to suggest that his eyes had rolled accidentally. He said he had been concerned about how other people perceived him, and he would never have wanted to hurt someone's feelings or alienate anyone with behavior so bold. At the same time, he was worried that others would read his thoughts—exposed when he rolled his eyes—and disagree or disapprove.

Another manager admits that she isn't always aware of what her eyes are doing. Sounds funny, doesn't it? But when you're thinking hard about something, you may not be conscious of your mannerisms. She says that one time, in the middle of a meeting, she rolled her eyes and sighed dramatically. A silence ensued. After a long and uncomfortable moment, someone asked her what the problem was. Acutely embarrassed by her "outburst," she explained that she had been thinking about something totally unrelated to the subject at hand. So, rolling eyeballs are not always a direct response to what's going on.

People with backbone understand this. They don't overreact to gestures. When they notice them, they watch for other signals to interpret what's going on. By contrast, people who lack backbone come unglued when sighs and rolling eyes make their way into the midst of things. They immediately wonder what they did wrong and how they can make amends.

Sidelong glances are more sophisticated. They reveal who has sided with another, who is providing quiet support, who is challenging a presentation, and who is just looking around self-consciously. How can you differentiate? When someone is in concert with another, a sidelong glance will often be accompanied by a subtle nod of the head, a raised eyebrow, or a gentle smile. Another tip-off is the look in the person's eyes as he makes eye contact. This look will convey agreement, concern, arrogance, disgust, even panic. By paying attention to what has just been said, at whom the person casts a sideways glance, and the message in that person's eyes, you can often gain useful insights.

When someone is providing quiet support, a sidelong glance is usually accompanied by a smile or a nod. When a position is challenged, the glance may include a curt movement of the chin toward the chest or a jerk of the head toward the speaker. A frown is common. Sometimes eyes roll at the end of the sidelong glance as if to say, "How ridiculous."

When someone is glancing around rapidly with a furtive look, chances are good the person is nervous or self-conscious. Oftentimes, these people are awaiting their turn to speak and have been mentally running through their presentations. With their glances, they may be counting friends and foes.

Half-mast eyelids—the expression Garfield made famous—can signify several different responses or conditions: boredom, lack of interest, lack of sleep, or overwhelming disdain for an idea or dislike of a speaker. Some people are born with heavy lids, so the appearance can be deceiving. This look is difficult to interpret without greater knowledge of the person.

How Light Plays

The light in people's eyes can tell you a lot about how they're feeling. Happy, sad, excited, bored, or even sick—the quality of brightness is revealing.

What do I mean by light? The magnitude of shine, sparkle, and activity. When people are excited or engaged, their eyes will be lively. They will reflect an inner enthusiasm. They will follow you, watching for signs to help interpret the meaning of what you're saying. An enthusiastic person's eyes may seem more intense; the eye color will be deeper and clearer, and their attention will be sharper.

Conversely, a disinterested or bored person's eyes will appear dull and flat. The sparkle and shine are missing, and the intensity of attention is markedly diminished. This person's eyes will not follow you; they may be downcast or staring into space. You may have the feeling that while this person's eyes are open, they're not receiving any inputs, and the brain is a long way off.

Anger, especially when held in check, glitters from people's eyes. There may be a smile on the lips (notice how tight the face is) and gracious words, but the eyes will blaze defiantly; you just know that someday in some way that anger will seep out.

Understanding how light plays is immensely useful. You can deduce who is onboard with your new idea and who couldn't care less. If you have a functioning backbone, you'll avoid the dim bulbs and seek out the sparklers.

By marking the light in people's eyes, you can frequently get a good emotional reading of a situation. This is important because when the heat is on, emotions drive all kinds of decisions.

Several years ago, eight managers were trying to come up with a compelling mission statement for their technology. This was at a time when mission statements were a sine qua non to the creation of shared vision and values. The group thus struggled mightily for something that would capture the firm's innovative spirit while corralling their great diversity of offerings into a portfolio that would be easy to describe and understand. Try as they would, no set of words seemed to resonate with everyone or represent clearly what the firm aspired to.

The debate centered on the difference between what clients would understand from the statement and what internal people would understand. One executive stated matter-of-factly, "Our clients won't care what our mission statement says as long as we have one." As he spoke, his eyes were cold and hard. There was no light coming from within, and the external light in the room was reflected back flatly. He held his head taut, and you could see the tension in his jaw and neck.

An alternative view came from another executive, who was quietly adamant in his opposition. His words were polite, and his manner was mild, but his eyes glittered with contempt as he asserted that the mission statement would be a rallying cry for confused and disillusioned workers throughout the firm. He was looking at the first guy who spoke. Uh-oh.

It appeared that them was fightin' words, and the discussion abruptly changed from the cre-

> We are as much as we see. Faith is sight and knowledge. The hands only serve the eyes.
>
> HENRY DAVID THOREAU

ation of a mission statement to an emotional analysis of what was wrong with the company and why people were so unhappy. Lines were drawn, and people took sides. Some eyes flashed; others hid. In the span of a minute or two, the room had erupted with bottled-up frustration. The CEO was dismayed and discomfited by this sudden volatility, and he quickly instructed the group to stick with the assignment at hand. He had drawn curtains over his eyes, so it was impossible to tell what he was thinking.

When the group met again several weeks later, the two protagonists gave each other a wide berth. Their camps had formed around them, but while the mission statement was being crafted, they avoided any further airing of company ills. The CEO presented a gruff exterior as he insisted that the mission statement issue be settled expediently, but attentive folks knew he was uncomfortable investing energy and resources in mission when bigger fish threatened the health of the firm. A dearth of backbone made everyone feel uneasy and fearful. They minced words and trod softly. Too bad.

Within two years, the infrastructure of the company began to crumble. Several large accounts were lost; some of the firm's best talent left in search of greener pastures (or more coworkers with backbone). The bigger problems so staunchly avoided came home to roost. The CEO was bounced, and the firm was restructured, then downsized. Today there's a mission statement, but few constituents know what it is or what it means.

Was all of this predictable simply by noting how people's eyes lit up or grew cold? Of course not. But several facts were apparent by watching the eyes of the people in that room. Strong emotions were being held in check, with a resultant high level of tension and strain. If only someone with backbone had let loose, the problems might have been resolvable.

The room held aggressors and victims. (This is normal.) Alliances were strongly signaled through eye contact, as were subtle warnings about how far to take things. People with backbone read signals like these and use them to gauge next steps. And those, by the way, are not sidesteps.

Where was the backbone here? Buried. Political expediency was the excuse that "strong" people gave for not demanding that core weaknesses be confronted—not only in this meeting, but ever. Who, after all, was going to step forward when the CEO was so tentative? You see it all the time. People who think they have backbone find out for sure in these kinds of situations. And believe it or not, eyes tell the story. When someone meets a challenge eyeball to eyeball, you know that backbone is engaged.

As you start catching on to eye language, be skeptical of snap interpretations. Put your eyeball observations together with other information before you conclude anything. Otherwise, you may be dead wrong.

That happened to Jeff one morning as he delivered a routine report to his boss and got an intense and irritable glare in return. Assuming that his report had alarmed or angered his boss, he asked what was wrong.

"Nothing," barked the boss. "Continue." He did, but he was sick with the thought that he'd said or done something he'd be sorry for.

Later that day, Jeff ran into the boss's secretary and asked what was going on. "Oh, nothing out of the ordinary. His kid took the car last night and brought it home with nothing but fumes left in the gas tank. He ran out of gas on his way to work this morning." Distraction and irritation had been clearly visible in the boss's eyes, but the reason for them had not.

Does Jeff have backbone? Nah.

Here's a backbone homonym you can use. People who lack backbone often Observe and React (OR). In Jeff's case, the boss glared, and Jeff got scared. Observe, react.

People with backbone introduce a middle step. They Observe, *Ask*, React (OAR). If Jeff had backbone, he'd have pressed his boss for clarification, perhaps saying something like, "You look upset. What's up?" He'd have gotten the explanation, then decided that life could comfortably go on. Observe, ask, react.

When you face little discomforts like these, you can choose OR or OAR. With OR you stay in the same place, observing and reacting, flipping and flopping, backing and forthing with your emotions. With OAR, you move forward, observing, asking simple questions, and reacting to practical information. Think of putting your OAR into the stream of life and using it to propel you in whatever direction you choose.

Incidentally, a lot of little OR moments add up to a major case of the wimps.

When Curtains Get Drawn

You've seen it happen. You'll be talking to someone, having a nice conversation, when all of a sudden, the other person "leaves." His or her eyes aren't focused on you anymore, although they may still be pointed at you. You wonder what happened.

When I worked as a copy manager for a marketing firm, my boss's office was right next to mine. From time to time, as I walked by, he'd call me in, asking how a certain project was going or what my schedule was for the day. I'd tell him, relaying details in an informative and entertaining way. After a certain period, which differed every time I stopped in, he would lose interest in what I was saying. He would still be looking at me, but I could tell he was no longer "there." The first few times this happened, I was uncomfortable and wondered what I had done to turn him off. Then I started watching him a little more closely.

When he was no longer interested in listening, an invisible curtain would descend over his eyeballs. The light in his eyes dimmed, and it was as though he retreated with his thoughts inside his brain, leaving me to talk to his vacated body. I was curious about whether he was paying any attention at all when this strange leave-taking occurred, so I began to experiment. Sometimes when it happened, I'd stop in the middle of a sentence and walk out, thinking that if my action seemed in any way strange, he would ask me about it. He never did. I'd change the subject abruptly: no reaction. It became clear that when those curtains were drawn, his attention was elsewhere. His eyes were open and he was still facing me, but his mind was someplace far away.

My point in experimenting like this was to watch my boss's actions and reactions as told through his eyes. From it, I surmised several things. One, that even though he asked me how a project was going, what he really wanted was some light conversation, a break from what he'd been doing. Two, that continuing to provide information after he had tuned out was an exercise in futility and future frustration. I was invariably asked again for the same information, regardless of how eloquently and completely I had already provided it. Three, that such leave-taking was not personal. It was not a judgment of my conversational expertise, my deftness in providing pithy information, or anything else having to do with me at all. It was simply his way of checking in and checking out, and something I had to learn to understand and watch for.

Others experienced the same phenomenon but interpreted it differently. Some thought he was arrogant and rude. Others thought he was a fool. Still others thought he was so far above them that he was easily bored with their commentary. These people spent a lot of time worrying about how they could do things differently to impress him and earn his respect. Nothing they did changed his actions. It couldn't. His behavior in this regard had nothing to do with them.

Their wonder and worry were backbone corrosives. They approached him (and probably others) with uncertainty, and they shaped their ideas and opinions to match his attitude. What a waste. He wasn't there!

Some people are accomplished at drawing a veil over their expressions, or putting on a "poker face." You'll see this a lot when discussions carry high stakes or when emotions run strong. When situations get tense, watch for curtains being shut. This will tell you who is still with you and who has opted out.

When you continue to talk in such situations, you are in danger of giving away more information about your position or desires than you should. If you notice that key players have drawn curtains, wind down your remarks. If someone pushes you to continue, say you need to gather your thoughts or reconsider your position thanks to some information shared earlier in the meeting. Don't keep talking!

If you notice that support people have drawn curtains, but the decision makers are still paying close attention, press on. Capitalize on the attention from the top, and use it to your advantage. Don't worry about the staffers; they can find out later what happened and what they need to do about it. Concentrate on the reactions of the decision makers. See what their eyes are doing. Are they agreeing with you? Are they checking things out among themselves?

People with backbone are attuned to moments like these in ways that others are not. People who have weak backbones may still gauge what's going on, but they'll do it in a more general sense. Drawn curtains distract them, and they get anxious when they lose anyone, regardless of decision-making stature.

How Eyes Connect and Reject

One of the easiest ways to see how the troops are aligning themselves is to watch the eyes. People who want to be in sync with one another will either make frequent eye contact or catch each other's eye, hold it for a split second—long enough to flash agreement—and then not check back again. Obviously, if you miss this connection, you may never know who is in silent agreement with whom.

People frequently seek eye contact during presentations. A speaker who is representing a group will often look at another group member for support. Watch for telltale communications in this exchange.

See what happens when a controversial subject comes up. The people who are least certain of their positions or power to influence the dialogue tend to look around quickly or not at all. These are the ones who study the ceiling with intensity. If they do look around, their eyes dash about the room, checking for agreement or disagreement. No backbone here.

By contrast, those who feel more secure in their positions will case the room more slowly and may lock briefly on someone who is nodding agreement. Their eyes are clear and calm, hallmark of backbone that's engaged.

By learning to watch and interpret eye language, you'll begin to see alliances and the lack thereof, levels of comfort and confidence, and how speakers draw energy from their audiences. You'll also gain insight into who's running the show.

Using Your Eyes to Advantage

Knowing that savvy people look for evidence of alignment or contention, you can use your eyes in purposeful ways. You can catch someone's eye to register interest. A quick glance says you get it. Add a smile to the glance, and you'll invite a question or comment directed at you. Smart people who want a speaker's attention attract it in this way. Really good, experienced people can actually direct a discussion and influence a speaker's remarks through skillful eye work.

Want someone to ask your opinion? Show interest with direct and friendly eye contact. Want someone to know that you couldn't care less about what he or she is saying? Avoid eye contact. Likewise, you can dismiss someone who catches your eye. Machiavellian managers love to punish subordinates in this way. You've seen people deflated like this, haven't you? The withering glance is a popular silent scourge. But it's effective only with weak victims; folks with backbone brush it off.

There are many ways to use your eyes. You can challenge people by gazing directly at them or holding their eyes for a few seconds. This is a good way to say "I disagree," without actually interrupting a discussion.

Asking a question with eyes wide open portrays innocent interest and friendliness. Most people are flattered to be approached in this way, and as you know, flattery works. Especially with backboneless folks. If you can sustain this wide-eyed posture, you stand to gain almost unlimited amounts of information. People with backbone use this type of eye contact for that very reason, but they do so judiciously. The downside of the wide-eyed look is that it can impart an airhead impression.

If you want to create distance, avoid eye contact. Don't feel like joining a discussion? Don't look up. But then, don't expect to be considered a player in that conversation, either. Not prepared to share your thoughts? Don't feel like meeting someone? Don't want to acknowledge that ridiculous remark? The easiest way to stay out of the fray is to keep your eyes to yourself. But remember that avoiding eye contact effectively takes you out of play, so use the technique sparingly.

To get good at using your eyes, pay attention to how others use theirs. Watch where eyes go, how quickly they travel, where they slow down, and where they stop. Ideas cause eyes to move. Words and emotions do, too. And color, and sound, and you name it. You can tell when people are actively using their analytical tools and when they're passively taking things in. Purposeful eye work telegraphs confidence.

It also makes a lot of people uncomfortable. Eye contact can be tough, and deliberately watching eyes takes a certain amount of emotional fortitude. Not everyone can do it. If you've been one of the queasy ones but you'd like to be a little bolder, an excellent way to practice in private is to watch movies. Great directors use eyes to convey nuances of meaning, emotion, and thought.

Black-and-white oldies are superb for this purpose. Charlie Chaplin was a master at creating full-fledged hilarity strictly through the use of his eyes. Alfred Hitchcock directed eyes to make our skin crawl. Lucille Ball, one of the grand dames of comedy, had the knack of absolutely denying the words she spoke by rolling her huge, expressive eyes. And when she turned them on Ricky in tender supplication, he didn't stand a chance. There. What a great reason to watch *I Love Lucy* reruns. Vaudeville acts and modern chick-flicks are rich resources, too. Action movies? Not usually, sorry. OK, OK. Sometimes there are scenes between exploding buildings and wild chases in which actors exchange meaningful looks. The gist is that when you are attuned to eye language, you can find it anywhere people interact.

People with backbone not only find it but also study it and learn how to employ it to their advantage.

BACKBONE-BUILDING EXERCISES

- ### *For Competence*

While you're perfecting your weekend couch-potato act, pay attention to actors' eyes. See if you can pick up nuances you never caught before. Watch for mismatches between words and eyes.

Watch people's eyes during meetings. See how many times someone gets "the look." See whose eyes are active and whose say "tilt." What's going on?

Get cable, and watch old movies. You'll get superbly eyes wise, and you'll laugh like crazy, too. And of course you know that laughter is excellent medicine.

- ### *For Confidence*

Keep track of how accurately you read people's eyes. When someone zings you, check the eyes. If there's a twinkle there, chuckle and let it go. If not, prepare for battle.

Pick someone you know well, and practice reading his or her eyes. Ask for candid feedback. If you're misreading eyes, it's important to understand how. And best to hear it from a friend.

- ### *For Risk Taking*

Practice using your eyes in different ways. Open them wide and ask a simple question that you've been a little afraid to ask. See what kind of answer you get.

Disagree in silence. Establish eye contact with the person who differs, and hold it. See what happens.

The same applies if someone baits you. Look directly at the person and hold both your gaze and your tongue. Let the other guy blink first.

Ex   .tract
You   Jhange

THE ABILITY   ffectively—is essential to the building   . Most people go through life thinkin   because that's what they learned, and so far, it's served   ell. They use the unrelenting pace of life and the confusion of changing mores as excuses to cling to tried-and-true mental models.

While this might be OK in social situations, it doesn't wash in business. To survive and thrive in an increasingly challenging world, you need to jump-start that backbone and rev up your mind to think more powerfully.

> It is not enough to have a good mind. The main thing is to use it well.
>
> DESCARTES

It's hard to change the way you think. It's a little scary sometimes, and the uncertainty that rises up when you step off of traditional platforms can cause you to retreat into old habits. The fact is that a lot of people just don't know how to think well anymore. It's even tough sometimes to know what you're thinking *about*. Work, family, health, hobbies, investments, cars, bills . . . all of life's particulars swirl around in your head like the bright bits of color inside a kaleidoscope. Every time something new passes through, the bits rotate and a new pattern appears. Multiply this phenomenon by hundreds or thousands of times each day, and it's easy to see why so many of us live in a state of vague or vast confusion.

Thinking is an art. And it's a tough one at which few people have the patience to do well. But if you hope to wield power and influence at work, you need to get serious about thinking. Specifically, you need to establish two habits. The first is to expand your thinking horizon by increasing the number of information resources you use. You need to read more broadly, listen more widely, and investigate more expansively. Then, after scanning a broader landscape of information, you need to narrow your field so you can think deeply and carefully.

Expand and contract. It sounds like a dichotomy, and in some ways it is. But it's essential to learn how to do this well. Good thinking is vital to the building of competence. It supports growing confidence. And it gives you the wherewithal to take intelligent risks.

Three main varieties of thinkers can be found in most organizations today. The first are those who seem to let thoughts and ideas seep into their minds, slither around the various brain lobes, then dissipate as innocently as they came, leaving behind little evidence that they existed at all. You can tell these people by looking into their eyes. You'll see vacancy or a look of mild, but not at all disagreeable, confusion. These types are frequently overwhelmed with the pace of change and the volume of information available to them each day. Their defensive response appears to be a disengagement of certain brain functions. They shelter themselves from the negative aspects of stress by appearing to take things as they come. Little seems to bother them; actually, little seems to register with them.

Beware of these people. They are without backbone. They will agree or disagree with ideas and proposals for whatever reason comes to mind, but they will just as soon forget what their position was. When it comes time to follow through, they're predictably unreliable.

Members of the second category of thinkers practically send out electric sparks generated by brains that churn thoughts and ideas in a swirling intellectual cauldron. They visibly react to new ideas. Their eyes follow speakers like laser beams. They twitch, blink rapidly, and seem to physically absorb and digest new ideas.

These people can't get enough of new things. They are in a state of continual motion. The more they see, the more they want to see. Their frenetic energy feeds on itself, driving them ever faster in the pursuit of knowledge and success. These are the Ricochet Rabbits of the work world. (You know, that cartoon character who was constantly bouncing off of hard surfaces and chortling, "Bing, bing, BING, I'm Ricochet

Rabbit!" He was an annoying little guy who, by today's standards, would probably be diagnosed with attention deficit disorder.) With all their energy and intellect, these people struggle to put things into perspective or to concentrate on one idea long enough to do anything about it. They may have backbones, but they sure don't take time to use 'em.

Somewhere in between these types are the folks who seem to collect new ideas like playing cards, waiting patiently until they have a near-full deck. With a good assortment in hand, they calmly spread the cards out on the table to see what they reveal. Are there patterns? Is there a preponderance of one kind over another? Are they related in any obvious ways? Are there connections that could be made, and if so, what might these connections yield?

This group may appear to represent an ideal thinking profile, and in many respects it does. However, even among these down-to-earth, patient, broad-range thinkers, you'll find uneasiness, a fear that time is passing them by. Their methodical approach to new ideas precludes their involvement in the best of them. Sometimes while they're collecting a certain set of cards, a new deck has been introduced and the game has changed. Oh, hang on to that backbone . . .

Strong strategic thinking skills are of prime importance to successful businesspeople. So, too, is concentration, especially when it comes to making an important decision. Given unlimited time and space, you might feel confident that you could excel at both. But everyone knows that there's never enough time in a business day to think as much as you know you should. You gotta be fleet on your feet, quick with a response, and always moving forward. Thinking—deep and serious thinking— only drags you down.

You might sense a note of facetiousness or sarcasm there. Good catch. Many executives complain that if they'd had one more day for review, they might have decided a case differently, and the outcomes of their decision might have been more positive. When I hear this sad lament, my question is always the same: Then, why not take another day?

Indeed. Why spend stores of energy to make decisions with which you're not comfortable, when a mere twenty-four hours might change the course of history?

Many businesspeople, confounded by overwhelming volumes of information coming at them nonstop from print, broadcast, and technology sources and battered by unrelenting pressure to decide *now*, have become paralyzed.

Life today is just plain complicated. And if you don't have a way of keeping track of input and thinking in an organized fashion, you're in deep trouble. But you already know that. So, let's look at some ways to structure and direct your thinking.

Mind Mapping as Warm-Up

Mind mapping is an excellent warm-up exercise for your brain because it helps to empty out what's crammed into your cranium. Once it's out, you can organize it. For comparison, take the junk drawer in your kitchen (or garage or office). This is where you toss the little things that don't have their own designated space. Bits of string, bolts, slim boxes of pencil lead, ticket stubs from that great play you've promised yourself you'll see again. You know the stuff. And you know what happens when the junk drawer gets on your nerves. You dump it out, sort what you want to keep from what you can now throw away without feeling sad, and put things back in a more orderly fashion.

Mind mapping does the same for your brain when it gets junked up with too much stuff. Mind mapping also helps you enhance the information you want to keep after you've sorted and organized it. In that regard, it's a great tool for personal brainstorming.

The process of mind mapping is simple. You write a word or phrase that describes the problem on which you're working in the center of a sheet of paper, then draw a circle around it. Now you let your mind roam free, and you write down all words, phrases, names, ideas, and thoughts that are triggered by your key word. You don't worry about whether there's any association between your key word or phrase and others that come to mind; just write them down. Even people with wobbly backbones can do this well. There aren't any censors.

But when you're finished with this portion of the exercise, you do have to make some decisions. Looking back over your work, you have to decide what words you can group together and where you can draw lines between entries that are associated in some way. You have to distinguish different groupings and figure out what shapes to draw around them or what colors to make them.

Here's how Harry, a marketing executive, used mind mapping to think in broader terms about a new product launch. He started with "new toy" in the center of his paper. In just over a minute, he had listed FAO Schwartz, stuffed toys, pet net in the kids' room, SpaghettiOs, consumer research, strike fast, great margins, big bonus, vacation trip, production capacity, best customer segments, regional demand, new suppliers, packaging colors, kids' TV programming, distribution channels, profit contribution, and test markets.

He then wrote "customers." That yielded rich, stingy, crabby, demanding, slow payments, missed shipments, forgot to return that phone call, angry now, nice letter from Bernice, thank customer service, call ABC company, get report to the COO, customers want more new products/fewer traditional ones, R&D needs research from marketing, focus group next week, are these effective?, demographic studies, missing key markets, customer mobility, spending patterns, listening posts, no more surveys!, no telemarketing!

Last, he tried "competitors" and came up with a list of toy makers, games, TV programs, electronic games, videos, and sports equipment. He also penned the names of several of his personal competitors at work and even a few childhood rivals.

As Harry reflected on his lists, he was struck by the breadth of what he'd produced in such a short time. He's competent, by golly, and liking that very much! (Now he's got some energy going. You can almost hear the backbone click into service.)

It's baffling how your brain works. One minute you're thinking about the business (competitors, distribution outlets, and profit margins), and the next you're thinking like a kid (TV shows, pet nets, and your favorite toy store). Guess what. This is exactly how innovation happens. If you can let your mind go and then record without censorship every thought that whips by, you'll find an incredible wealth of experience, emotion, wisdom, even all kinds of technical stuff that you probably don't remember learning. This is great backbone-enriching material.

> **Freedom of speech and freedom of action are meaningless without freedom to think. And there is no freedom of thought without doubt.**
>
> BERGEN EVANS (1904–1978), AUTHOR, *THE NATURAL HISTORY OF NONSENSE*

Your challenge as a business thinker is to harness the energy and expertise housed in your brain without getting all tangled up in a mental melee. Mind mapping allows for unhampered and undisciplined free association of thought, with the assurance that by writing everything down, you can go back to sort, categorize, and make sense of what you produced.

What do you have when you've completed a mind-mapping exercise? A funky-looking drawing of where your brain took you. That's interesting and entertaining, but if you stop at the map, you're missing the power of the exercise. Now you need to study the map. Find out what other areas connect to the original thought with special relevance. Incorporate these into your thinking. Be mindful of the ties, and figure out why they exist and how you might develop them further.

Mind mapping helps you take that first step toward better thinking, namely, understanding what you're thinking about and why. It's a great tool to identify and prioritize your preoccupations.

Big-Picture Pieces Expanded

Through mind mapping, you're likely to realize that several important concerns are competing for mind space and attention. List them and rank them. To help you establish priorities, go back to your big-picture map. Try to determine which pieces impinge on your current scenarios. Ask yourself a few operative questions: What are the primary big-picture elements involved? How are they related? Who else has a stake or a hand in this situation? What can influence the outcome?

When Harry identified his big-picture pieces, he saw that finance, distribution, and package design were among them. He also realized that he needed to understand sales dynamics as they relate to the timing of the launch. Consumer and market research had already been done, but in somewhat of a vacuum. He suspected that results of his focus group studies might look different with production and distribution information added to the mix.

As you expand your big-picture pieces, conclusions will dawn on you. Harry ascertained that he needed to add detail about where his customers are and aren't. He had made some big assumptions about this and suddenly wasn't so sure those assumptions were valid. He needed to be more aware of what customer feedback the company has, how they get it, how valuable it is, and how well they use it. This suggests a few more lines on the big-picture map, showing interaction among groups, including advertising, marketing, and customer service.

Harry's big-picture map also doesn't show any connection between engineering or production and customers, yet customer feedback should be a prime source of information for those two functions. Looks as if a few components need to be added there, too.

If this seems like a whole lot of tedium to you, you're not alone in you thinking. But time invested in this kind of work is essential to building backbone. Realizations like these gave Harry concrete direction. In the past, vague notions about the business floated around in Harry's mind, which in turn created uncertainty and a wishy-washy approach to his work.

Dan, an automotive import executive, reflects on this fact of business life:

> How do we do our homework on a subject? We tend to gather facts superficially to support our position. But if we were to truly watch and listen in order to understand what we're dealing with, we'd be better prepared. We'd be able to handle unanticipated events. We'd feel stronger about our thoughts and freer to discuss our position. We'd respond more intelligently to questions and challenges. And we'd be better informed to accomodate change further down the line. I don't think we'd be slowed down. In fact, by paying attention and learning about a situation, we'd be better equipped to act with dispatch and confidence.

Sounds like backbone.

Each time you gain information or benefit from an insight, make a note of it on your big-picture map. By incorporating this detail, you build your knowledge bank. That's competence, and accumulating it in a wide range of business transactions gives you the backbone to tackle problems straight on.

What are you struggling with now? What are the primary elements? How are they related? What details in the mix are extraneous or irrelevant to the substance? (Lots of stuff is nice to know, but what do you need to know?) What implications ride with this information glut? What if you do nothing?

Are you suffering backbone paralysis?

A Question of Time

So many questions and so little time. Which brings us to another task: determining your decision time line. Not every decision needs the same amount of reflection. (I know, duh.) But a lot of mischief is caused when people identify themselves as "quick" or "careful" decision makers. It's as though they have only one method (and time frame) for making decisions, regardless of the nature of the decision itself. If the problem at hand is chronic and has serious implications, your decision time line is likely to be different from that for a problem that's urgent but not crucial overall. (It had better be.)

Your time frame sets parameters for your research. It may, for example, limit the number of links you can choose from a host website. It'll determine whether you can dig into relevant big-picture pieces to understand hidden connections or make only a cursory check of them for obvious relationships. It'll dictate how much "continuing education" you can absorb on your way to your decision.

Contrast a decision regarding the selection of a new director of technology, for instance, with a decision on software upgrades. Both have potentially strong implications for the success of your organization, but one is likely to be more urgent than the other.

Identifying the elements involved in a situation, gathering information about them, and then connecting the dots to create an understandable scenario take time. Sometimes a lot of time. This is where many otherwise qualified businesspeople fall off the effectiveness track. Many are reluctant to carve out the time required to think well. Many have bought the notion that visibility and volubility are the roads to executive success. They're wrong. Attention, discipline, and good solid thinking are far more direct.

Prism Action: How to Train Your Focus

All right. You've identified precisely the dilemma you're thinking about. You've tapped relevant big-picture elements and made some fundamental connections. You've got boatloads of good, even great information.

Now what? How do you sort through it all and sharpen your thinking in a way that helps you reach a good decision?

Admit it. You're looking for a guarantee that the information you select and apply to your current situation will make you "right." Forget that; there is no such guarantee. There is no right answer. People without backbone can't get this into their heads. They say, "Yeah, sure. I know," but then they burrow back into the problem, stubbornly determined to find it. People with backbone know that while there are no right answers, there are effective decisions.

Go back to your problem. What, specifically, are you trying to figure out? In the new-toy-launch dilemma, Harry wants assurance that the toy will be a smash hit. There's no way to predict that. But what will constitute success: a certain sales volume? a net profit contribution? an expanded market share?

Typically, the answer is all three. And this is what leads to so much fuzzy thinking and wibble-wobble decision making. If Harry can buck up his backbone long enough to decide which of these constitutes success, he can begin to hone his thinking.

You may still want to argue that they're all important. Fine. Let's look at it. Will a set sales volume guarantee a net profit contribution? No, and the reason is that there are too many uncontrollable variables. Stores can discount the suggested retail price to move product. Sales representatives can make mistakes on volume discounts to stores. Theft, defective merchandise, goods lost in transit . . . these and heaven knows how many other glitches can influence profitability despite sales volume.

> I'm a victim of my business school education. I was taught to put my faith in spreadsheets and research and decision trees and simulation programs. The more data I could collect, the smarter my decisions. My professors never told me I'd be flying by the seat of my pants.
>
> ENTREPRENEUR

How do you track sales volume, anyway? Who provides the numbers? How valid are they? And how, by the way, are sales bonuses determined? You see the traps. People with weak backbones get drawn into arguments about these subjects all the time. Focus? What focus?

But back to Harry. For each of his potential success factors—sales volume, profit contribution, market share—the properties of the decision are different. Interrelated, yes. But different enough that the thought process changes. At risk of grossly oversimplifying, let's assert that sales volume hinges largely on production capacity, marketing effectiveness, and retail seasonality. Get one of those three big pieces wrong, and sales plummet. Profitability is impacted by production capacity and quality, pricing policies, and distribution. Market share correlates with product innovation, competitive presence, and breadth of sales channels.

Are we splitting hairs? No, we're not. If you don't understand the contributors, you're not going to solve your problem. Period. Just as a prism transforms a beam of white light into its multicolored elements, you can refract your situation. Understanding the individual parts and how they fit together is requisite to making solid, workable decisions about the whole. Lazy thinkers with lazy backbones whine that it's hairsplitting. That's why they're so inept at effective thinking and decision making.

When you can train your focus and refine your thinking, it'll allow you to see business problems in actionable steps. It'll give you a fighting chance at exercising your backbone.

Extraction Techniques

OK, you've applied prism to problem, and you now have a clearer, tighter bead. You also have an impressive collection of data from magazine articles, opinion pieces, business reports, government-issued projections, statistics from the World Wide Web, customer surveys, executive mandates, competitive comparisons, interindustry comparisons, and last month's financial statements. If only you had time to read it all, not to mention interpret and use it all!

Add to this burden our societal preoccupation with who is doing what to whom, why, when, and what it means to fans worldwide, and it becomes clear that you teeter at the edge of near-hopeless collapse under trivia. How can you possibly keep up with the pace?

You can't.

And because you can't, you have to learn how to extract what's important, setting aside what's merely nice to know for a quieter day. Maybe a day long after you're retired from all this excitement. Extraction is a backbone activity. You gotta pick some facts and ditch some facts without always being sure of your choices.

You can do this in several ways. Start by clarifying, once again, what you're thinking about. Do you need to decide *whether* to do something, *how* to do something, or how to *finance* something? You're definitely thinking about something, but what do you need to determine? Have a purpose for your thinking. Any information that doesn't work toward your purpose is, at least for the moment, extraneous.

Figure out which of your many information sources are best. Go for substance over style. When you get a report, look first for the executive summary. If there isn't one, ask for it. Don't waste your time plowing through reams of material. Get the main points. If you want to investigate something further, make note of it, and gather only the additional data that assist your investigation. It's too easy to get sucked into details and lose sight of the real story. Don't be afraid to reject reports that don't tell you anything meaningful, regardless of how prestigious they are or how impressive they look. People with weak backbones shiver at the thought of rejecting high-profile stuff. They might miss something!

Find and listen to credible advisers. Seek out those who have broad knowledge and experience as it relates to your situation. Listen for a variety of examples and applications of ideas, as opposed to one big thought expressed seventeen different ways. And incidentally, don't believe everything you hear. Yes, I know you know this, but with so much expert opinion flying around, it's worth a reminder. Take what you hear with a large grain of salt and a healthy measure of perspective.

Recognize, too, that as you extract bits of information, you're going to leave a lot on the table (or in cyberspace). This is good! It's necessary. You should be able to justify why you leave what you leave. Keep that backbone engaged, and remember: You're thinking about something for a specific reason.

Shucking for Mental Health

With wave upon wave of fast-breaking, headline-making, profit-impacting information, shucking is a survival skill. Shucking is a two-part technique. The first is throwing away what you don't need; the second, deflecting stuff before it hits you.

Shucking differs from extraction in its wholesale aggressiveness. You don't carefully select; you shuck! See that pile of six-month-old business magazines? Shuck it. Yes, I know there are some useful articles in the stack, but you get a host of more current ones each month. The longer those old ones sit there, the more you worry about reading them. Those anxious thoughts junk up your mind and corrode your backbone. See those boxes of year-old customer surveys? Skim off a dozen samples at random, and shuck the rest. Those automatic E-mail reports you get each day whether you have time to read them or not? Save one or two of value, and shuck the rest. Shuck routine where it no longer serves you. Shuck time-wasting phone calls. Shuck association memberships that you've outgrown.

Feeling nervous? That's your backbone telling you it's a little weak. Good thing you're working on it.

Shucking requires an ability to think in multiple time frames and dimensions. What are you doing now and where are you headed in the future? How will changes in your industry impact your career? What new opportunities will arise, and what skills will they demand? If you want to be a forward-thinking and long-lived professional, you need to track trends to the future while fortifying yourself with enough current news and views to keep you successful in the meantime. There are major chunks of information that you'll never need. In fact, there are whole categories of data that you'll probably never know about. That's fine. If it doesn't serve your purpose, shuck it.

Getting to Yes . . . or No

All thinking has at its end a goal. Should you or should you not do something? Should you or should you not say something? Should you or should you not make your move?

Should you continue to investigate an idea, or relegate it to your future-great-opportunity file? Should you fix a long-standing problem, or leave well enough alone? Should you raise your hand for help, or tough it out? Should you accept a challenge, or wait for a better time? Should you fire someone, or move him to another spot in the company? Should you take responsibility, or turn a blind eye?

And the $64,000 question (drum roll, please): Will you or will you not exercise your backbone?

BACKBONE-BUILDING EXERCISES

• *For Competence*

Get a handle on your thoughts. Dump out that mental junk drawer and sort through what's there. Throw away old stuff, and organize what's left.

Prioritize your thinking. If there's an urgent decision to be made, set aside other concerns to give it undivided attention.

Figure out what goes into the nice-to-know and need-to-know categories. Concentrate on need-to-know stuff.

• *For Confidence*

Keep track of where your mind goes, and capitalize on the journey!

Refract your dilemma. Investigate the elements. Poke around in the big pieces to see what you can snap together.

Recognize that the "right" answer doesn't exist.

• *For Risk Taking*

Take time to think. This'll be tough sometimes, especially when rivals and skeptics taunt you by saying, "If you knew what you were doing, this wouldn't take so long."

Practice shucking. Shovel out your office. Compress your Internet files. Take expert opinion with a grain of salt. Who cares if everybody else watches and listens to "everything"? When others go down under the weight, you'll be riding high.

Make independent judgments! Aim for a decision, and stay on track, even when weak-backboned rascals try to distract you.

Associate on Purpose

BIRDS OF A feather flock together. It's one of those annoying clichés that make us wince, but it's true. And though we sometimes like to turn away from the truth of clichés, if we are to be of strong backbone, we must learn to face it.

This is a sensitive chapter because it deals with who we are (and who we think we are), who others think we are, and how in the world to reconcile differences in a way that lets us sleep at night. I guess you could call it the clash between "to thine own self be true" and "perception is reality."

How much of yourself do you want to tinker with on the way to a strong backbone? How much do you really need to? These questions deserve some special consideration.

> **Tell me thy company, and I'll tell thee what thou art.**
>
> CERVANTES

David was the opinion leader in his close-knit group of software developers. He was the guy who always asked management for more and better software tools, bigger and better projects, and faster and straighter answers. David liked being the rebel spokesman for his group because he knew they needed one and because he liked the limelight. David had aspirations. He wanted to be promoted to a management spot because he wanted to shake them up and shake them loose from some stodgy mind-sets.

David got his wish. He was made the information systems (IS) manager for customer programs when the company divided its technology group into internal and external solutions experts. One part of the group was given responsibility for the company's infrastructure, while the other was charged with developing and implementing client programs.

David's associations at work changed after his promotion. His former coworkers were now his direct reports. He spent the lion's share of his days in management meetings. Though he was smart as a whip when it came to software, he sure didn't understand much about management. He suffered the classic adjustment pains that often accompany promotion: uncertainty of his capabilities in the new role and loneliness at having left his former circle. He even started dressing more conservatively to fit in better with his new management peers. David's friends started referring to him as one of "them." He was judged by his associations.

We all are. And whether we like it or not, how we handle this particular reality will have a lot of bearing on how successful we are at growing a backbone.

Associations can be Achilles' heels. We can talk all day about how good we are at what we do and how despite that, we recognize our need to improve, but when the subject turns to whom we pal around with, we get a little testy.

The fact is that although diversity has birds of very different feathers congregating these days, most people like to spend time with others who are like them: people who think along the same lines, wear similar clothing, go to the same church or grocery stores, read the same books, like the same kinds of movies. For the most part, they don't examine why they like what they like. They just do. And they're not real comfortable talking about it, thank you very much.

People with backbone like what they like for reasons they understand and accept. They acknowledge that others' tastes and preferences may differ and are OK with that. They recognize, too, that others will judge them for better or worse based on where they see them congregate. They're OK with that too. Their strong backbones have come partly as a result of their facing up to disagreement and sometimes disapproval.

They are who they are, and that's that.

If you're going to have a strong backbone, you've got to understand your preferences and accept that others will base their impressions about you on your choices. If those people are important to you, you'll pay attention. If not, you won't.

Many of our associations are based first on accidents of birth. Where and to whom we were born imprints us with these early connections. Where we grew up and went to school established fundamental values and sometimes lifelong friends. If your family was mobile, you may have a larger worldview and greater comfort with variety than someone whose family always lived in the same neighborhood.

In a similar way, job skills and attitudes are frequently shaped by early work experiences. Where you live impacts what you do by virtue of what kinds of jobs are available in your area. From the day you are born, you become what you are around. This can be rich soil for excuse making, and people with weak backbones who don't like where they are in life tend to till it. People with strong backbones have better occupations.

You Are Who You Hang With

Strong people tend to hang around with strong people; weak folks hang around with wimps. Success hangs around success; failure with failure. Happy with happy; gloomy with glum. Look around you. Evidence is everywhere.

Olympic great Carl Lewis advised, "Realize that you are not supposed to lower your standards to meet people. You are supposed to encourage people to come up to yours. Otherwise, you have nothing to do with them. You should shoot to be as high as you possibly can and then demand that people around you be at that same level."

This is a big backbone deal. If you've got the guts to pursue a dream, don't you want to be around others who understand it?

Lewis's words can be misconstrued in ways that are harmful. Taken on the surface, having "nothing to do with" people who do not meet your standards can be twisted to mean that you need not bother extending a helping hand, that on your own personal journey the needs of others should be shut out. This is not, of course, what he was saying. Rather, that's a view of the world that comes from spineless people—the victims who seem to be everywhere these days. Lewis's comments go to the singular determination required to build extraordinary competence in your work of choice. In other words, hanging around with people who drag you down is a waste of time, energy, and potential.

Gary, an art director for a Minneapolis ad agency, said over lunch one day that he'd concluded over his long and challenging career that people come in two basic varieties: energy givers and energy takers. He said that in order to be at the top of his talent and do breakthrough work for his clients, he needs to be around energy givers. Anytime he has an important challenge in front of him, he strives to avoid energy takers. He can't afford to be dragged down. This presents difficulties when he has to engage with energy-taking subordinates and clients who demand his time and attention. But after a particularly bad day, which he says he can always attribute to energy takers, he'll try to load his schedule the following day with energy givers.

Whom you associate with at work tells others a lot about where your head is in terms of accomplishment and ambition. And about how you think you can get to where you want to go. The political realities associated with organizational upheaval have altered how some people associate, and there is danger here. Political alliances don't necessarily deliver on the promise of advantageous alignment. Even when they do, it's a pretty ephemeral hook on which to hang your hat.

A former Fortune 500 chemicals company executive with twenty-five years' experience described how relationships at work changed when the company headed into a major transformation. Senior managers recognized that the old-line company needed to remake itself to adapt to the fast-changing business environment, but they were uncertain as to the best way to proceed. They were keenly aware of worker restlessness and distrust as the workforce was reshaped.

As the former executive points out, when acquisitions like the one he experienced occur (his company was purchased in 1998), employee performance is often judged on a short time horizon. Some mid- and senior-level workers who had been with the firm for twenty years and more were assessed based on the last two or three years of effort. Because of this, he said, interpersonal relationships and personal advancement became much higher priorities for managers than the refinement of any specific competencies. A lot of otherwise smart and accomplished people started worrying more about whom they know than what they know. Curious how a game of musical chairs can dissolve backbones—or reveal that they were never there in the first place.

With all the business shake-ups going on, how secure do you feel when a new management team moves in? Probably not very, even in the best of circumstances. But with some measure of competence and self-confidence—a backbone—you'll feel stronger and better able to maneuver through whatever circumstances arise than if you had marginal competence and a boatload of insecurity. With developed competence in your line of work, you have value to contribute to a firm, and whether you survive a restructuring or not, your skills enable employability. If you rely instead on political connections as your foundation, you're at the mercy of whims; depending who your friends are, you may or may not be welcome elsewhere. But those are dire circumstances.

In a more routine work world, it's natural to slot yourself into places in which you feel comfortable. You visit with certain people during breaks, seek out friends during meetings, and have lunch with folks you like. Think about this. Why these people? What makes it comfortable? When I ask executives this question, a common reply is, "It just feels right to me. I feel as if I belong."

But why? As you work to develop a healthy backbone, you need to ask yourself: Are you comfortable because you are accepted for who you are, with no questions asked? (This is the most common response to the question.) Because you understand the lifestyle and language of your group? Because you share common interests or worldviews? Because you can hide?

Become conscious of why you choose to hang around with cer-

> **A friend to everybody is a friend to nobody.**
> SPANISH PROVERB

tain types of people and not others. Going with the flow is fine if you want to stay where you are. But if you're interested in growing and advancing yourself, you must become more finely attuned to your choices and your habits. If you can put your finger on what makes you comfortable in your favorite groups, and line this up with where you picture yourself at your best, you'll be pointed in the right direction.

Recognize that when you join a group, you're judged as part of it. Your personal identity disappears, and you become "those people." This can be advantageous for you when the group you join is viewed positively by people who are important to you. Think of the professional associations to which you belong. Didn't you choose them because of their prominence? Their good reputations?

But group membership can be not-so-good, too. Groups of teenagers strike fear into many adult hearts. Why? Because many adults think teenagers dress weird. They act weird. They pierce their bodies in unthinkable places. They talk goofy. They're loud. They're full of raging hormonal energy, and that makes a lot of people nervous. Consequently, judgments are typically negative.

But viewing teenagers in a group makes it hard to see and appreciate any one individual. As you assess the group, so too do you assess all the individuals. Is this fair? Of course not. Does it happen? All the time.

Why is awareness of this tendency important? Because where and with whom you spend your time can have an impact on how much power and influence you wield at work. Whom do you hang with? What kind of reputation do they have? Make sure you have it straight. People with backbone don't whine about being misjudged.

Creeping Meatballs

Back when I was a kid, adults used to refer to unsavory characters as "meatballs." I was amused by the expression because it was kind of cute and very benign. Years later, my peer group called unsavories "hoods," or "greasers." Every generation has its own unique label, though I have to plead ignorance to today's.

At any rate, "creeping meatballs" is an expression used by Glenn, a vice president of automotive marketing. He used to observe certain individuals in his company who would wander the halls together, sit near each other in meetings, and grab center stage in whatever fashion they could, embarrassing or otherwise.

In his estimation, they were "meatballs" because they were shallow minded, ego driven, and narcissistic. They were "creeping meatballs" because they had the propensity to seek each other out. Drawing a whimsical picture for comparison, Glenn said, "Imagine a big plate of spaghetti and meatballs. As the spaghetti is consumed, the meatballs tend to creep toward the center of the plate. Soon, they're the sole focus of the diner's attention. The same thing happens with human 'meatballs.' They creep together and move toward the center of attention.

"It's funny to watch them bump into each other," he said. "Instinctively, they push away, but upon realizing it's 'one of them,' they grin and make room. Over a couple of hours, you can have quite a collection of creeping meatballs, all happily entertaining each other. Very little business gets done, but they have a terrific time together, and they use similar expressions. 'Don't know' is sometimes shorthand for 'I don't know what you're talking about. I have no information. I was unaware of the matter.' Alternatively, 'Don't know' means, 'I understand what you're talking about, but I'm not the expert, and I'll lose the stage if I offer my thoughts, so I'm not going to waste my time acknowledging you or your request.'"

Creeping meatballs come in a variety of flavors, and they're easy to recognize because they all lack backbone. They take comfort in numbers and specialize in groupthink. Anytime you run into people who have to check what they think with their associates, you know you've encountered creeping meatballs. Escape quickly.

And be alert to trappings of your own group memberships and habits. Groups exert pressure to conform, and it's easy to get drawn into situations or actions you might otherwise reject. You'll need a strong backbone sometimes to march to your own drummer.

Marianne knows this all too well. She's a board member and long-time supporter of a local youth club. She's well known in the community for her association, and because the club is also well known and well regarded, the association reflects positively. When guns in schools became a hotly debated topic nationwide, Marianne found herself at odds with several of the club's most active board members. She couldn't believe it when she saw them transform into creeping meatballs, hungry for the community spotlight and their proverbial fifteen minutes of fame.

The creeping meatballs sponsored community meetings to discuss violence in schools. The meetings drew wide attendance. Participants were vocal and emotional. The creeping meatballs loved it! Swept along on the passion of the moment, they publicly supported policies with which Marianne adamantly disagreed. They advocated shutting down schools when threatening phone calls came in or when graffiti were found somewhere on the school property. They endorsed installing metal detectors and armed security guards. Marianne held that the club could be much more helpful by working with kids in their structured programs—sports, field trips, educational sessions—than by getting in the middle of administrative and political hassles involving the schools.

Marianne presented her views at board meetings, but the majority overruled her. When the club started getting negative press in the community—ironically, for the very reasons she had voiced—Marianne found herself tarred by association. Being of strong backbone, she calmly explained her differences to those who asked, but otherwise refused to get lured into public debate. She also refrained from saying, "I told you so."

Why Associations Are Automatic

People judge quickly. They see something—an accident, a speech, a hurried exchange—and, as it registers somewhere in their consciousness, they immediately decide essentially what happened and who the good guys and bad guys are. Police reports from accident scenes are maddening because witnesses to the exact same event often have opposing perceptions about what happened.

Don't you make snap judgments? We all do. Why? Because there is so much going on around us at all times that to stop and rationally determine what happened and who was responsible is beyond our ken.

When people see you with others, they make assessments on the spot. Many times, initial impressions are faulty. Sometimes you have opportunity later to change them, but for the most part, people see you and draw inferences about you.

Complicating matters, when people make such judgments, they are often driven by their own psychological state at the moment. If someone is crabby and happens to notice you in a group of people with whom he or she is not friendly, you will be damned by association. Fair? No. But it happens all the time.

Knowing this, what are you to do? And what does this have to do with building backbone?

Automatic association falls into the fact-of-life category. There is nothing urgent for you to do except to be aware of the tendency. If, however, you are unhappy with the determinations being made about you, you can choose to be more careful of where and with whom you appear.

As far as building backbone is concerned, your choosing is the determinant. You have several options where automatic associations occur. You can choose to remain oblivious to them. (You're nuts; this doesn't happen.) You can choose to be aware of them but ignore them. (Don't bore me with facts.) You can choose to be upset by them and continue to associate with the same people you always have, despite the negative reflection on you. (It's my life.)

People with backbone choose to be aware of their associations and sensitive to how the associations impact their reputations. When the impact is harmful to them, they risk change. They also allow plenty of time and space for this change, and they brace themselves to deal with hurt feelings—theirs and others'.

Weak-backboned people scoff at the idea of quick verdicts. After all, your track record should count for much more than any happenstance finding. In theory, it should. In practice, it doesn't always.

Automatic associations can be damaging and even fatal to your long-term reputation. Of course, they can be markedly positive, too, as Lisa found to her pleasant surprise. Lisa was a new recruit to a fast-growing software development company. Her coworkers were all young and ambitious, and she loved the fast pace and animated dialogue she had with her colleagues. She was a little less aggressive than some of them—didn't like to toot her own horn quite as loudly—but she held her own, technically. Her boss was older, a mentor to the group, and influential in the industry. He was also an active champion of his workers. Lisa got an out-of-the-blue phone call from a client one day, profusely praising her work and thanking her for the time she dedicated to his account. The client added, "Your boss, whom I have tremendous respect for, said wonderful things about you at our meeting last week. He's a smart guy, and by the sound of his praise, I'm sure I'll enjoy working with you."

If your associations make you look better than you think you are, appreciate them. Realize, though, that if you weren't as good as you are, these people wouldn't bother with you.

But there is a nasty side to automatic associations, and you need to be cognizant of how they can hurt you. People with backbone accept life's nasties and maximize the profit from the experience.

The CEO of a publicly traded applied technology firm had a sidekick who had followed him from company to company throughout the careers of both men. (This is not necessarily bad. Look at the Lone Ranger and Tonto. Batman and Robin. Butch and Sundance. Oh, no. Strike those last two.)

In prior firms, the CEO had been a senior exec but not the head guy. In most instances, other executives had noted the relationship between the man and his sidekick, but because the tagalong was relatively unobtrusive, they joked a bit about it but chalked it up as a nonthreatening executive perk.

He that lies with the dogs, riseth with fleas.

GEORGE HERBERT

Until now. With CEO responsibilities and direct reports jockeying for position, the sidekick became an obstruction. He was a tough guy; unsophisticated and, at times, alarmingly crude. He also had an uncertain background, having followed so closely on the heels of the CEO for every position he'd held. What value did the guy bring to the table? How did he get to be where he was? And why in heaven's name had the CEO dragged him along all these years? These were the questions on the minds of the other managers.

Emboldened by the fact that his buddy was now top dog, the sidekick grew downright outrageous. He routinely swore at subordinates at top volume and once, in a fit of rage, trashed a computer. When a brave exec dared to complain about him, the CEO shrugged it off. Pointed to his "good work." Said the guy was a soldier and his loyalty was important to him.

If you've ever led through great turmoil or change, you can sympathize with the CEO's desire to have a trusty lieutenant. It is lonely at the top. Had the CEO exerted a little backbone to suppress his sidekick's shenanigans, people might have cut them some slack. But he didn't. And they didn't.

Stung by the implication that an unsophisticated coattail rider was privy to inside information to which they were not, several of the senior-level executives sought greener pastures and greater respect. People with backbone move away from bad situations, especially when they're powerless to change them. Those who remained began silently opposing the CEO at more and more junctures. (Spineless creatures.) As the CEO's sphere of influence dwindled, he became thin-skinned and defensive. No backbone here, as you already know. If the CEO had a backbone, he wouldn't be hauling a rummy around with him.

At any rate, the company's performance tanked, and the board stepped in. When the CEO got the boot, so did the sidekick.

Though this result was not strictly due to an automatic association, as word spread about the unsavoriness of the sidekick, many who did not know the CEO assumed he was as bad. Birds of a feather. Creeping meatballs. Spineless ones, all. With little time or inclination to understand more, the automatic association—and judgment—was made.

Why Good Is Better

Here's a quiz. Would you rather be seen with tall people or short people? Fat people or skinny people? Nice people or mean people? People who look alike or people who look different? People who look athletic or people who look sedentary? Colorful people or conservative ones? Animated or reserved? People with body piercing or without? People with highly styled hair or more natural 'dos? Smilers or frowners? Joke tellers or headline readers?

I'm asking these questions to tweak your awareness. Hasty determinations happen all day every day. You will see and be seen, judge and be judged, based on information that is incomplete and, probably more often than not, incorrect. Sometimes people will "know" that what you're doing is positive; sometimes they'll decide it's not. If there is a ratio of right-to-wrong estimations, I don't know it, but it's fair to assume that at best it's an even split.

Be aware of automatic assessments. Do what you can to ensure that the lion's share of snap judgments made about you are positive. Why is good better? Because it saves you the need for explanation, justification, and rationalization. Anytime you find yourself saying, "I'm not really like the rest of them," you've got potential trouble.

People with strong backbones make good associations on purpose. They hang around with people from whom they can learn, people who make them laugh. By the way, people with backbone laugh in appreciation, not derision. The only people they laugh *at* are themselves.

People with backbone associate with people who can give them straight feedback. They don't have time for back scratchers or butt kissers. They associate with people who tell the truth. Who are happy when they succeed. Who can put them in touch with others who can teach them. Who keep their promises, no matter how small.

People with backbone associate with people who let them rant and then gently point out why they're wrong. Who tell them bad news even when they're nervous about how it'll be received. Who understand mistakes and forgive them when they make one. But only, of course, after they've explained what went wrong and how to fix it.

People with backbone hang around people who can admit they're afraid sometimes, who refuse to hike down the pity path even after life has kicked them in the teeth, who like to work hard and who love what they're becoming as a result.

There are also a bunch of folks who people with backbone stay away from. Those who look down their noses at others. Who prey on the weaknesses of others to advance themselves. Who lie. Who can't explain themselves when they disagree with others. Who cave under pressure. Who insist on relaxing when the job remains unfinished.

People with backbone avoid people who don't like someone "just because." Those who resent others' brains, beauty, money, energy, possessions, relationships, life.

People with backbone avoid people who tell others they just don't get it. These people don't give explanations, just rejection.

People with backbone stay away from people who are rude. Who hit or throw things. Who belittle others. Who haven't changed their thinking in the last five years. (This is generous, by the way.)

People with backbone don't associate with people who say no as automatically as they breathe. Who don't trust laughter. Who make others feel stupid or small or silly because they dream big dreams.

You get the picture. People with backbone hang around with folks who can help them be strong and happy. Energy givers, as Gary calls them. They stay away from negative, manipulative, lazy, or mean people who drag them down. Energy takers.

To grow a strong backbone, make good associations. Spend time with people who are attentive to the business. Listen to conversations; where discussions center on how to solve problems, improve relationships, or otherwise move the business forward, get involved. These are the people whom others are likely to respect for their dedication to positive change. Recognize that some of these conversations will be very animated, even heated. Strong opinions frequently lead to contentious exchanges. Passersby might mistake this energy as negative. But as people expound on what went on in these meetings, the content will assume center stage, not the personalities. Besides, you know that the participants in discussions like this are likely to be found at other times shaking hands and extending friendship to each other.

Diatribes that rage about who did what to whom and who found out about it later are a waste of your time. Banish them.

Always extend respect and courtesy. Always. Even when you're toe to toe with unpleasant people and situations, pledge yourself to respectful behavior. When situations flame up, your calm demeanor will tell others that you're in charge. Where the other people involved might be known as troublemakers, and your association with them might cast aspersions on you, your respectful, controlled presence will set you apart.

Associate with people who care for themselves. You know who they are. They dress well, speak well, and go about their business with self-assurance.

Recognize that the kinds of people with whom you are most often seen will create an image of you that others carry in their minds. When someone hears your name, what comes to mind?

As you consider this question, think too about making good associations a priority. In some cases, this may mean significant change to your routine, but the payoff in building backbone and being seen as someone important is worth the trade.

How to Disconnect from Habit

As anyone who has tried to quit smoking, begin an exercise routine, or carve out more time to read knows, breaking old habits and creating new ones is hard work. It demands attention, determination, diligence, and stamina. Where personal relationships are part of the package, there is also likely to be some pain. As you begin to consider changing your associations, be aware of the strong possibility for this discomfort. If you expect it, you can better assuage it.

John is a foreman for a printing company. A man's man, all tough external masculinity. Calloused hands and a callous manner that belie his huge, tender heart. John chews tobacco at work, aiming graceful arcs of juice at the spittoon next to his press. He talks straight, scratches openly, and has the most colorful language in the industry. The guys love John.

An after-work ritual had grown up with the guys over years of working together. Every day at quitting time, they headed for the corner saloon to have a few beers and tell tall tales. John was always the center of attention.

But John wanted to do more with his life. He wasn't sure how to break out of his comfortable patterns, or even where he was going, but he knew he didn't want to be standing at the printing press for the next thirty years. He was an avid reader, and many of the business magazines he perused told him to take charge of his future.

He did. Quietly, he found a mentor, a friend of the family who had done well and for whom he had great respect. He also found a coach through a contact at a local industry association. Both told him that if he wanted to grow beyond where he was, he'd have to start spending his time differently. Fewer visits to the saloon, more attendance at industry seminars and networking meetings.

John struggled in his recast role. He felt strange in new groups. Self-conscious. Out of place. He missed his old routines. The guys at work started razzing him about getting a little big for his britches. John second-guessed his own ambition on more than a few occasions. He loved the guys, and he felt bad about leaving them behind as he headed toward his future. But his backbone was sturdy. He realized he had to make his own way. The guys couldn't do it for him. And the life they had just wasn't enough for John anymore.

To create his new life, he had to change his associations. By doing so, he began to think about different things, look for different opportunities, and test himself in ways that sometimes made him apprehensive. This is the way of backbone. It's not easy, and sometimes it's not much fun. But the payoff in growth and satisfaction is rich.

When you want to disconnect from habit, have a purpose in mind. What do you want to be like? How do you want to use your brain? What do you want to accomplish? Set goals in relationship to your answers to these questions. Start with small steps. Find someone to help you. Even the strongest and most motivated backbone developers need encouragement and support. No man is an island, remember?

Create a strong, positive image of yourself, and hold it close. Be realistic in this! I know a man who wanted desperately to be an outgoing, compassionate, and charismatic leader—one who demanded excellence but allowed for learning curves and sincere effort. As an idealized image, it was great. But it didn't match at all with who he was: a quiet, introverted man who had no experience in the spotlight. His desire to build a backbone was vague—a wishful, wistful longing. And because he tried to do it privately—didn't want anyone to know what he was working on, in case he failed—he didn't stand much of a chance to succeed.

When you picture yourself successful and strong, be specific about the features of the image. Do a reality check, adjust as needed, and then get busy.

If you're hanging around with people who think ambition is a dirty word, disentangle yourself from them. Anyone who has given up on learning and growth is trouble. Complacency is not your friend.

Associate on purpose. It will help you build backbone of a very important kind.

BACKBONE-BUILDING EXERCISES

• **For Competence**

Pay attention to the judgments you make of other people. Stop and ask yourself why you hold particular opinions: What forms the basis for your assessment?

Each time you judge someone in a group, recognize that you are making generalizations that may not be correct. Appreciate that others do the same about you.

Watch how people at work congregate. Are there observable similarities among members of the fold? See if you can determine what unites them.

• **For Confidence**

Listen to people talk about groups of which they're not a part. Understand that idle gossip, though part of the workaday world, is often like background music or white noise; few pay close attention. Still, when you are the subject of such chatter, listen for its substance. If there is none, let it roll off, and go about your business. If there is, pay heed.

Associate with people who get the work done. Not only will you learn a lot, but you'll also be pegged as a positive contributor.

Follow your own growth agenda. Examine old habits, and honestly assess their value. Commit to move past those you've outgrown.

Take care of yourself. Eat well, sleep well, dress well. Your self-image has a lot to do with how confidently you stand up to the judgments of others.

• *For Risk Taking*

Make like a fish: choose your school, and swim. If you find you're with sharks and you'd rather be with dolphins, move on.

Start weaning yourself from time- or energy-wasting associations of habit. Take a different route home from work to avoid old hang-outs. Make a date with someone influential to draw you into positive associations.

Invest in your future. Create the self-image you want instead of going along with what your crowd has assigned for you.

Play Columbo

PETER FALK PORTRAYED an unforgettable character in Columbo, the rambling, disheveled, and seemingly disorganized sleuth. Columbo was wise like a fox, though, and in the end, he always got the bad guy.

Not to characterize business dealings in terms of good and bad guys, or to strike a blow at John Malloy's *Dress for Success* admonitions, but a study of Columbo provides keys to developing power and influence in your professional life.

Questions work better than statements. Unless you are the undisputed authority in a given situation (even then), and unless you are certain that you have all relevant facts in hand (when are you ever?), asking a question opens the door to discussion and discovery in a way that making statements cannot. Statements shut down inquiry, discovery, and oftentimes innovation. Statements convey finality. See?

> It is better to know some of the questions than all of the answers.
>
> SAYING

Some people argue that this distinction is only a matter of style. Rhetorical questions sound like statements, after all. In fact, they are intended to be; by definition, a rhetorical question is one "asked merely for effect with no answer expected."

Think about the statements you make. How many times have you wished you could rephrase or rescind one? Foot-in-mouth disease strikes without warning. Do you believe, as many do, that speaking authoritatively conveys decisiveness and command? That making statements is a sure route to greater influence? Wrong. Imagine Columbo proclaiming all over the place. People would have quickly tired of hearing his "expert" opinion. They'd probably have started tuning out as soon as they heard his voice. So much for the show, in that case. And so much for Columbo's success in nailing culprits.

In a competitive, complex business environment where even slight advantage is hard to come by, wise denizens know that statements are stultifying. Proclamations do not collaboration, exploration, or innovation make. People with backbone celebrate the invention of questions. They use them freely and creatively to crack open the windows of insight.

The Art of Asking Questions

The ability to ask insightful questions is a multipurpose backbone tool. What do you know today that you didn't know before because you asked someone something? From another standpoint, what have you asked yourself lately that led to self-discovery or realization? How you ask a question will often determine whether or not you get the information you're after. Columbo had the timing down pat. Just when people thought he was out of their hair, he'd ask an insightful and usually unsettling question. The effect was powerful. He also exhibited a rumpled and innocent manner that was disarming when, of course, he was shrewd and anything but innocent.

You can learn to have the same effectiveness. (No, it doesn't start with tossing your ironing board onto the scrap heap.)

Skillful questioning blends a keen understanding of issues with sensitivity to the intensity of the debate and a sophisticated sense of timing. If you have a solid understanding of the issues, why would you ask questions about them? For several very good reasons. You might, for example, ask to verify the currentness of your beliefs. Things change. What was true yesterday might not be so today. You can ask questions to establish a sense of collaboration with others. Though you may be the recognized authority on a subject, questions invite others to share their viewpoints and perspectives. You might hear an angle you hadn't considered. Or learn something of which you weren't aware. People with backbone savor these situations.

You can ask questions to get a feel for where there is common understanding or to find out where confusion exists. People with backbone use this technique to guide discussions in a way that's beneficial for everyone.

You can also use questions about subjects you understand to intimidate and embarrass. Hecklers with tunnel vision are effectively stymied when you ask a pointed question. Though you won't want to adopt this as a daily routine (people with backbone don't abuse others), using questions to deflect opponents and bring off-base hecklers back to the subject is a handy backbone skill to have at your disposal.

Let's examine a few situations to see the advantage of the well-tuned question.

Helen is a senior project manager for a large industrial parts manufacturer. She works with companies from around the world and routinely contends with time and geography differences. Because of this, she is always on the lookout for technologies to help her communicate faster and maximize profit from her efforts. When several of her business contacts enthusiastically recommended a groupware package that she had heard about, Helen didn't hesitate to examine it. After rigorous personal testing, she was convinced that the product would enable her to collaborate more effectively with her customers and business partners, and to keep closer tabs on competitive activities as well.

Helen was recognized within her company as an informal techie—someone with an excellent grasp of how new tools could be integrated with existing ones to the company's best advantage. She was enthusiastic about the new groupware and felt strongly that her company should add it to its current technology portfolio. In fact, Helen had been asked to chair a meeting to discuss this recommendation.

She was also aware that one of the IS guys favored a different solution. Jeff is a systems analyst who had joined the company two years after Helen did. Jeff had a certain amount of influence, especially with a group of users who were unfamiliar with the tool Helen championed. Acknowledging this informal influence, Helen had met with Jeff on several occasions to discuss her groupware solution, and though he didn't agree with her assessment, he was willing to participate in a formal discussion about it. Prior to her meeting, Helen gave careful thought to winning Jeff's approval.

Why should Helen care about Jeff's approval? If she believed that the tool she was recommending was the superior solution, why worry about what Jeff or anyone else might think? Because while the solution might be perfect, Helen knew that the implementation would require attention and effort from Jeff and many others.

How often have you done something by mandate and resented it? How different do you feel when someone asks your opinion and seeks to convince you in a way that respects your expertise and honors the challenges you raise? Having a backbone means recognizing the need to work with and through others. This, believe it or not, takes greater strength and savvy than ramming something through the system. It also pays greater dividends.

Helen began the meeting with a review of existing technologies. She described the current need that would be served by her groupware recommendation, taking care to acknowledge that there were other tools that could also meet the need. She pointed out that Jeff favored another product. "Would you like to share your insights with the group, Jeff?" Of course he would.

As Jeff delivered his presentation, Helen watched the reactions of others in the room. Where they reacted favorably to Jeff's comments, she made a note to leverage this positive response in relationship to her tool. Where they expressed confusion or doubt, she noted how her solution might satisfy them. By the time Jeff finished, Helen had an outline that made a point-by-point comparison possible.

But rather than declaring her assessment of what Jeff had said, she asked if-then and good-better questions. The responses convinced her of four things: First, that Jeff's tool would work. Second, that hers would work better. Third, that regardless of which solution was chosen, the company would be better off. And fourth, that by approaching the situation with questions and an attitude of helpfulness, she gained support she might not otherwise have had. Helen's backbone set up that much-sought-after win-win result.

The meeting moved to the final phase: questions and summary comments. Consider this the bonus round where the real players become apparent. The rules are brief: Ask a question, you continue on; make a statement, you're out.

Helen scanned her notes and looked around the table. "Mary?"

"I don't think it'll support file sharing in the way I need it to." Statement! Mary's out. She doesn't *think* it'll support, but she doesn't know for sure. Why not ask?

Kevin says, "I have serious concerns about the security of your system." Another statement. Kevin's out. No place to go with that declaration, sorry.

Sally asks, "Are there significant differences in load time?" Good question; it's something to look at and compare.

Dave asks, "How much file space did you say it needs?" Dave stays in.

Ron says, "The supplier you're working with doesn't have much of a history. It's hard to judge how this is going to play long-term." And his question is? Ron's out.

Jeff had the technical advantage in this situation because his IS background commanded more automatic respect than Helen's project management expertise. As is true in so many firms, where you fit in the functional scheme of things often determines how closely others listen to what you have to say. But Helen had a broader and more sophisticated view of her company's overall operations and the backbone to ask and invite probing questions. She was able to convincingly demonstrate that her groupware solution held significant benefit for others as well as for herself.

Another instance in which the art of questioning can be invaluable is in determining the veracity | **Every why hath a wherefore.**
SHAKESPEARE

of sophisticated salespeople and consultants. Some are truly as good as they sound, but others are just as truly charlatans. How to tell the difference? Listen closely, with the recognition that just as artists use color and brushes to paint an image, poseurs use words and energy to create an image of sophistication and competence. Insightful but disarmingly simple questions delight pros and unsettle charlatans. Recall Columbo up against clever, high-profile opponents. He'd scrutinize them, scratch his head a bit, then turn an open face in their direction with a simple and direct question. They'd crack every time.

After hearing an eloquent dissertation filled with current buzzwords and popular sentiment, see if there's any way to plug them into your business and your current needs. Ask a thoughtful question. Get the speaker to clarify a thought or provide greater depth (if the person can). Watch what happens.

When you have the backbone to ask a truly insightful question, a charlatan will consider you the enemy. You'll see the brow furrow, dark clouds will gather across the person's countenance, eyelids will sink to half closed, and a suspicious, gloomy look will be turned on you. You'll be deemed a threat.

This is fascinating because at the moment you are neither friend nor foe. You are merely looking for greater explanation to understand a pertinent thought expressed by the expert. When the expert feels challenged by an intelligent question, your backbone makes you the victor. Maybe saves your company a bundle of money and precious time, too.

One other common and sensitive situation in which skillful questioning is a tremendous backbone asset is in asking for more responsibility or monetary reward. Most people mistakenly point to what associates are earning in their positions or what competitive firms are paying, and make statements about that. Salary surveys, headhunter reports, and all other manner of justification are often touted to support a request for advancement. This is a softheaded approach that's easy to deflect. I've seen one impatient manager end such a session with a one-word question. "So?"

A stronger, backbone-filled approach is to be armed with demonstrations of contributions you've made, a pragmatic assessment of areas in which you could make stronger contributions based on your skills and the organization's needs, and a supply of relevant, specific questions.

Such questions might include: "How fast do you want to move on that acquisition?" "What kinds of resources do we need, and how can I help?" "Would you like updates by phone, E-mail, or written report?" Queries regarding the speed or agility of known competitors are good. So are questions about the implications of moving either faster or slower than originally planned.

Prepare yourself by framing your goal in terms of how you can help your organization become stronger, more competitive, and more profitable. With this partnership attitude, make a list of questions. This will yield an approach that is quite different from and much more productive than the customary you-owe-me or you-are-lucky-to-have-me routines.

Why Approach Is Everything

There is much to be curious about at work: why certain decisions are made. Why some products are developed and not others. Why someone gets recognition or a promotion and others don't. Why suggestions go unheeded or, worse, bring on angry responses. Why projects stagnate. Why people don't return phone calls. Why reports are exaggerated or falsified. Why your idea was soundly praised in a meeting and then just as soundly ignored afterward.

When you want to know, ask. People without backbones mumble and grumble because "no one tells us anything." If they'd ask, they'd have more information and better dispositions. Better opportunities, too.

Consider this classic business scenario. Alan is senior vice president of marketing for a national leather goods manufacturer. Steve works for him. Alan asked Steve to put together a presentation of last year's ad campaigns, including sample ads and the costs of running them nationally, as well as total sales for the year, by quarter. Alan wanted to use the presentation, intended for the chairman, president, and other senior managers, to make a case for a bigger advertising budget.

Steve developed an imaginative presentation, pulling Alan's favorite ads and correlating ad expenditures to sales peaks. He wanted to show cause-and-effect (good ads mean strong sales) and entertain the guys at the same time.

Showtime. Steve rolled the ads, punched at wall maps showing hot sales spots, and generally played the savvy advertising guy to a tee. One problem: The ads he selected were the ones most disliked by the president. The president and the chairman got into an argument about what makes an ad effective. They wrangled over costs, babbled about reach, and took off on a journey into the maddeningly unmeasurable realm of proof of advertising effectiveness. A bigger advertising budget? No way.

Alan was livid at having lost control of the meeting and his request for more money. Steve was mortified. How was he supposed to know that Alan's favorite ads were the president's biggest pains?

Alan wanted Steve's butt (spineless folks, when embarrassed, get mean). Now the question is, Will Alan use effective questions, or will he make final-sounding statements? He's mad enough to fire Steve! Will he write Steve a scathe-o-gram about poor performance, or will he send a more reasonable E-mail message requesting a meeting with Steve in which he can pose a two-part query? (The two-part query might ask first, "In review, what was the objective of the meeting?," and second, "How do you think you did?")

If Alan had a backbone, he'd allow himself time to settle down, quell his emotional reaction, and meet with Steve. He'd ask the questions with intent to instruct. The discussion surrounding the "how do you think you did?" part could, despite the runaway-train effect of the selected ads, be valuable. If Steve genuinely thought he did fine, Alan might be justified in launching him. Otherwise, probing could surface some other good questions. Why, for example, did the president so dislike the ads? Should his negative reaction be taken into account for further ad development? How involved did Alan want the president in OK'ing creative?

Approach is paramount as you begin to practice asking questions. A question is a request for information. A statement is delivery of same. Sometimes when you raise a question, you want data. Facts. Sometimes you want interpretation or explanation of those facts. But whether you want one or the other, your question should have a defined purpose.

Columbo knew exactly what he was after before he asked a question. He didn't always know what the answer would be, but he usually had a strong hunch. He used questions to verify his understanding, straighten out items that didn't make sense, and eliminate pieces that just didn't fit.

Understanding your purpose before you ask a question greatly facilitates getting what you seek. Misunderstanding is rife in our abbreviated and compressed business world. You can use this propensity for misunderstanding to your benefit (Columbo did this too, with glee), or you can be frustrated and confused by it; by having a well-considered purpose in mind before making your queries, you hold the cards.

Christopher, a mid-level manager, was considering a new job opportunity with a large multinational. During the interview process, he met with several corporate executives as well as people in the local office. Here's his account of the process:

> I was impressed with their energy and professionalism, and I could envision myself as "one of them." But I was uncertain. What I do and am good at did not line up 100 percent with what the company does. As people were interviewing me, I asked each one of them to describe the company's main business. What products and services did they offer? Who were their best customers? How had the organization grown in the past? What were the chief reasons for its success?
>
> As you might imagine, I got a lot of different answers, depending on the positions people held and the type of work they did. They were positive or negative according to how successful they'd been with the firm. I suppose this is normal. But the degree to which the answers differed and the intensity of

some of the emotions made me uncomfortable. Besides that, no one seemed to have an integrated understanding of the business or any inclination to look to the future. They were parked in their individual positions and couldn't care less, really, about the ideas or opinions of anybody else, unless they happened to agree with theirs.

When I had a wrap-up meeting with my potential new boss, I asked him the same questions. I was looking for both facts and explanations. What products and services did they offer? Who were their best customers? How had the organization grown in the past? What accounted for their success?

When he talked about products and services, I noticed a definite emphasis on some more than others. This made me curious. I wanted to know why some were favored over others, and what this implied regarding the pace and direction of future growth. I suspected that traditional services received preference. I was right.

Christopher explained that the majority of the firm's professionals had been around for ten or more years, and they were skilled at selling and providing the traditional services. The firm's reputation rested on this. These people wanted to continue doing what they'd always done to ensure the continuing good name of the company. In Christopher's mind that made sense. But, as his potential boss pointed out, those services were now being offered by a growing number of competitors at prices that were squeezing their margins. That's why the firm was redirecting its attention and resources toward new services in different, but adjacent, market segments. That's why, in fact, they were interested in having Christopher join them.

He made a mental note: Part of his job was going to be assisting in a major change effort.

Next they talked about customers. Tradition figured strongly there, too. Many clients were long-standing and loyal, having developed relationships over the years that were both personal and professional. But this was changing as older customer contacts retired and younger people took over. Start-up companies and mergers of traditional firms were creating a whole new landscape. Cost pressures were getting more intense, which meant that the firm's traditional services were being scrutinized. He could tell that this irritated his potential boss, and he asked about it: "You seem disappointed by these changes. Why?"

In response his boss said that new (and mostly younger) clients didn't know what they were looking at. They didn't have any idea what good or bad quality is. They didn't respect the tradition of the business. How could they judge? They bought on price. That's why his people were so disgusted. They felt that standards throughout the industry were falling and that their best efforts were being wasted. He admitted that the energy and enthusiasm of his best people were waning.

Christopher made another mental note: The firm hoped for an infusion of new energy from him.

Additional questions about past growth and the reasons for it hit on the same subjects. Data showed a fairly undisturbed growth pattern and a stable workforce for nearly fifteen years. Changes in marketplace demand, competitive pressure, and worker availability made the old equation obsolete. As they talked about the future, Christopher sensed more tension and impatience. In fact, as his follow-up questions asked for interpretation of what the past meant to the future, he could see that his potential boss was feeling overwhelmed.

> He acknowledged that his success had come in a stable and predictable environment that he understood. He said he also understood why substantial change was called for now, but he wasn't completely comfortable leading it, given the cast of characters he currently had. He wasn't sure what kinds of new people he needed or even where to find them.
>
> My final question was the telling one for me: "Given all these demands, how do you see me serving the organization?"
>
> In a long, drawn-out response, I learned that what he wanted were my business contacts and sales skills. My familiarity with and interest in the new services they were considering was a plus, though he warned that new growth would probably come slowly and as a result of other efforts within the firm. In other words, I wouldn't be a driver. He wanted me to provide a short-term infusion of energy, new revenue, and a positive attitude toward change.
>
> As I thought about it, I decided that this company was headed into a period of painful change for which, in my mind, they were ill equipped. I had no doubt that I could be helpful, but I realized that anything I could do on my own would fall far short of what they needed to successfully navigate this change. I decided to pass on the opportunity.

Christopher had some kind of backbone here. Those questions!

And look what happened. Just like Columbo charging past the obvious and into the revealing, Christopher's questions enabled him to get to the heart of his concerns. They were direct and purposeful. Many targeted sensitive subjects, and he asked them with as much respect and sensitivity as he could. His matter-of-fact manner helped his potential employer feel comfortable enough to be unusually candid.

He got people to talk beyond pat answers, and as they did, he got the real story of what was going on. People with strong backbones insist on looking at the realities of new opportunities. They appreciate the sizzle— fat salaries and impressive titles—but they objectively assess their chances for truly making a difference.

Christopher's decision to take another post was prescient. Three people moved into and out of the position in one year. The company continues to limp along on traditional offerings. The new services were tabled.

In another instance, I was working with a company that was experiencing explosive growth and struggling to keep up with it. The firm enjoyed an excellent reputation in an industry that was undergoing transformation. (Aren't they all?) As is true for most companies today, technology had changed the way work got done and how people communicated with each other. Change brought confusion. Confusion engendered power struggles. People were tired and crabby, and some were even depressed. At the core of these struggles was a basic lack of infrastructure to support the business. This firm had no backbone! (Many of the people did, but the business itself did not.) A contributing problem was a subtle but growing identity crisis brought on by recent changes in leadership.

As we began to explore ways to "get things under control so we can grow even faster," I had a long list of basic questions. But I knew that if I laid my entire list on these managers, they'd probably collapse under the weight. (Wasn't that last camel-back-breaking straw unbelievably light?) How many questions can executives have fired at them, regardless of how sincere or motivated they are to figure things out? I started simply: How did work come into the firm? Who handled it internally? Who touched it first, second, third? We made a big-picture map and drew critical paths. This was good because we got a little silly with crayons and markers, and things didn't seem so life-and-death after a while.

We worked our way through major strategy pieces—customers, suppliers, resources, profitability of certain lines, viability of new opportunities. We asked simple questions (that were sometimes devilishly hard to answer!) designed to paint a clear picture of where they were and where they wanted to go. We played Columbo. And as Columbo always did at the end of his show, we reached logical conclusions and satisfying answers. We even had a few of those forehead-slapping moments when something obvious occurred to us that we'd missed before. By the time we were done, we had designed a company backbone, an infrastructure strong enough and flexible enough to enable opportunistic growth.

Most companies stop short out of frustration with questions that seem too complex or are too difficult to face. They take a live-or-die, gotta-operate-now mode to their self-assessment when a lighter, more exploratory approach would be healthier. People who lack backbone often look for quick answers. When they can't find them, they go hunting instead for excuses or scapegoats. People with backbone understand the advantage of getting to the end of the exercise with useful information and insight. They don't back off of tough questions, but they do gauge their own energy and capacity, and proceed accordingly.

Remember Columbo. He always had mission-impossible odds, but that's why he loved what he did. He always had a method to his madness, too. Adapt your behavior based on what you're trying to learn or figure out. Be sensitive to the attitudes of the people you seek to query. Cultivate your manner in order to capture every shred of information you can.

Timing Your Queries

Have you ever asked a question that set off a tirade? Or one that brought a tear to someone's eye, or that unleashed a flow of gratitude seemingly unrelated to your query? If so, you likely are acutely aware of the power of timing.

Some people believe that timing is a matter of luck. Sometimes it is. Most times, though, those who leverage clues from their environments tend to ask the right questions at the right time. Because they watch and think and prepare, they are . . . yep, backbone people.

Here's some backbone advice. Don't ask people questions when they're clearly upset or distracted. They'll have to stop their brains from spinning around whatever is bothering them to hear what you ask, understand what you're after, and then fulfill your request. Forget it. The best you can do in frenzied situations is quiet people down and let them spill what's riling them up. Your note-taking skills, honed in Chapter 3, will help you capture the overflow and sort the contents.

Another time you don't want to be firing questions at people is when they're thinking. (Watch their eyes; you'll be able to tell.) When pressured for results, many people make the mistake of producing a long list of questions—like the ones I had ready for my client in the preceding case—and firing them off in rapid succession. This becomes a futile exercise—a game show. You're the hyperactive host, shooting off questions while your poor contestant races to cough up an answer, any answer, to move on to the next question. How many useful answers do you suppose you'll get?

Stream-of-consciousness questions—those that pop into your mind because of what someone said—are confusing. Except in an animated social dialogue, they rarely have a credible place. Now, Columbo seemed at times to be wandering far afield with his questions, but in fact he had carefully surveyed his terrain and knew the lay of the land. His helter-skelter delivery was calculated to trap his opponents.

When you find yourself wanting to ask a barrage of wide-ranging questions, jot them down and organize them. Your big-picture map from Chapter 1 will help you link related questions and group others into logical categories. As you begin to ask questions, you can move from category to category, asking relevant, impromptu, follow-up questions during the discussion. By organizing yourself, you gain power to extract meaningful information.

> **Man can learn nothing unless he proceeds from the known to the unknown.**
> CLAUDE BERNARD

You'll also create an impression of attentiveness and professionalism. You'll exude backbone.

To keep backbone engaged, another timing tenet demands your attention. Some people use rapid questioning in chaotic situations to grab power. When others are clearly stressed, spineless opportunists will ask ridiculous questions to gain advantage. They know that what they're asking is unreasonable or wrong. They count on the likelihood that harried associates will not be fully attentive and will respond with whatever seems to make sense at the time. That ostensibly innocent gambit can be diabolical. These situations are dangerous because people who operate this way usually take care to note the "facts" of the exchange—a question was asked and you responded thus—to justify why they took foolish or forbidden action. Beware these circumstances! And remember to think when someone asks you a question. If you're not prepared to give it proper attention, say so. Naturally, you'll want to assure your inquisitor that you'll be happy to entertain the request at another time.

One final aspect of timing is in your control, because it concerns altering your normal habits. If you are famous for your never-ending questions, stop. Let several weeks go by without your posing a question. This switch will get attention. People will guess that your extended silence means you're thinking hard. For this reason, the next question you ask is likely to be heard more keenly. Make it a good one. If, on the other hand, you are a reluctant questioner, take the reins off your curiosity. Jot down items you wonder about, and organize them into categories that reflect your business. Engage your backbone to ask one good question in the next meeting you attend, and see what happens.

Daring to Be Direct

Columbo mumbled and fumbled around to create an image of hapless harmlessness. But when he asked a question, he came at it straight. He used his facial expressions and body positioning to soften the perceived directness of his query, but he went right to the heart of what he wanted to know.

That takes backbone.

How many people do you know who come right out and ask what's on their minds? Direct and relevant questions are pretty rare. (Because backbone is, too?) Direct and irrelevant or insulting questions, hallmarks of the backboneless, are shockingly common.

When Joe steals Ben's new idea and writes it up as his own, Ben asks Joe what the hell he thought he was doing. Ben knows full well that Joe wanted to cop the credit. So, his question is direct but irrelevant; it's a challenge to Joe's behavior that leads to open conflict. If conflict is what Ben wanted, his purpose is achieved. Of course, that's not the case. Ben wants to stop being taken advantage of, and he wants due credit for his ideas. But he doesn't have the backbone to address these objectives directly.

Tom, on the other hand, has been to the mat with Joe and held his own. Joe tried to borrow an idea of his once, too. But Tom had the backbone to face him head-on. He asked Joe specific questions about the idea. Using Joe's answers—nonanswers, actually—Tom exposed Joe's foolishness and retained the credit for himself. Tom's questions were direct and relevant to his purpose. The effect of this straight shooting is much more forceful. Joe will continue to steal ideas, but he'll think twice before ripping off Tom's.

Asking direct questions feels uncomfortable to a lot of people. This discomfort comes from two primary sources: either the questions that come to mind are not the right ones (you can feel this in your gut), or the person you're asking is unprepared to field them (you can read this in the person's eyes). It takes backbone to recognize the circumstance and decide how to proceed.

"Why did you do that?" is rarely an effective question. It's most frequently asked when someone makes a mistake, and it invites all kinds of feeble answers such as the maddening, "I don't know." What is the point of that question? If you sincerely want to understand what happened, ask, "What happened?" The explanation will often reveal the reason for the mistake. If you want to know whether the person who made the mistake is just plain dumb, the explanation will show you this, too. So "Why did you do that?," though direct, is the wrong question. People with backbone distinguish.

"Why is your report late?" is another simple and direct question that feels uncomfortable for some. It feels confrontational to the weak, but people with backbone know that it is actually a straightforward request for information. If the person receiving the question feels guilty about missing a deadline, he or she will be uncomfortable. That's OK. If the deadline was inflexible, that discomfort is good. (If the deadline was arbitrary, there's something else to hash out.) Asking why something is late is legitimate. And necessary. There may be a number of reasons, from uncertainty about how to structure the report or what to include, to competing deadline pressures from other work, to personal problems that intervened. People with backbone don't waste time speculating about these reasons. They ask the direct question and wait for a thoughtful response. This gives everyone something to work with.

Incidentally, I disagree with people who say there are no dumb questions. Of course there are. Dumb questions are born of sloppy thinking, inattentiveness, rudeness, and other unproductive habits. They escape

backboneless people with some regularity. But questions that reveal ignorance—a lack of knowledge about something—are not dumb unless
they go unasked. People with backbone never apologize for lacking
knowledge; they constantly seek to build it. That's why they ask direct,
purposeful questions.

Asking direct questions can feel inordinately risky, especially if you're
not used to asking much of anything. But when direct questions pertain
to the dynamics of the business and are presented in the spirit of genuine
problem solving and knowledge building, there is nothing more refreshing. They afford access to trouble spots and make room for serious and
concerted attention.

The Question Bin—Sample Questions for All Occasions

I hope the questions that abound in this chapter and throughout the book
have sparked more of your own. Business presents so many aspects worth
exploring that it's impossible to think about all of them at once. Your big-
picture map gives you a plethora of categories on which to train your
thinking. The notes you take can clue you into hidden intricacies of situations and relationships. Your observations of people and events precipitate other questions worth mulling. Here are a few more from the bin.
They're simple, useful, and important backbone builders. Think of them
as all-purpose greeting cards—the ones you use when there's no special
occasion but you want to stay in touch with someone.

Questions to Ask Others

These five questions help you get a handle on where people are.

Why? This is a perfect question for almost all situations that you
don't fully understand. (It's also a perfectly annoying question to people
with weak backbones. It scares 'em.)

When you ask it, keep your tone light. A heavy "Why?" with a som-
ber expression and tightly drawn eyebrows makes others nervous. This
thundercloud expression is a favorite of weak people—it makes them feel
strong—but people with backbone use it sparingly. That's because they

realize that asking why opens a door to understanding. When you ask why, you can learn how people reached a particular conclusion (and how they think), what resources they drew from (and what they pay attention to), how they implemented an idea (and how they go about getting things done). A simple "why" can unleash a wealth of information.

How do you know that? This is not a challenge! It's a request for information. Anyone who tells you something knows it *somehow*. Heard it from someone else? Read it in the paper? Heard it on the radio? Learned it from experience? Learned it in a class? Just made it up? When you ask how someone knows, you are seeking indication of validity. Not everything that appears in the newspaper or makes its way along the airwaves is valid.

What's next? Here's a perfect problem-solving follow-up question when the situation has been defined and everyone's thoughts have been mined. People with backbone love this question because it gives them a firm handle on who the players are. When prospective respondents don't have a clue or are afraid to venture what comes next, you know they're not players.

What do you think? This is a tough question for people with weak backbones. Of course they think something, but for them to put it out there for others to evaluate . . . whoa. That's scary. Applying this lesson to business, if you can't get someone to tell you what he or she thinks, you'll have little chance of working well together. Will you play mind games with Cracker Jack prizes when you guess right?

What will you do? This is a cousin to "What's next?" but goes more directly to an individual's plans. People with backbone like to kick this question around because in doing so, they usually discover barriers to some options and wide-open doorways to others. It elicits details concerning time line, resource availability, and quality of backbone required to take action. However, when they're dealing with people who have no spine, they get vague or meandering thoughts about possibilities and opportunities. They quickly move on.

Questions to Ask Yourself

The following questions help you reach a better understanding of your own mind-set, which of course fosters backbone.

Why? Good for the same reasons as stated in the preceding category. When you can push yourself to answer *why* you feel a certain way or want something or wish something would happen, you'll get powerful insights into what drives you. This is prime backbone-building material.

What do I think? If you're going to impose this question on others, you'd best be prepared to answer it yourself. When you adopt the habit of asking this question internally, you'll find lots of ready backbone to confront challengers. You'll know what you think! And why!

What do I want? When you know what you want and can articulate it, you'll understand the reasons why you think and feel the way you do. People with weak backbone often squirm from this question. It's difficult to answer sometimes. Fears about not getting what you want, getting it too quickly or easily, or getting it at the expense of other desires makes this a potentially stressful question. People with backbone think seriously about what they want and make plans and decisions based on the answer. This self-knowledge helps them stand firm when someone tries to get them to do (or want) something else.

What am I afraid of? Here's a potent question that few people like to ask themselves. Who wants to run around cataloging one's own fears? After all, everybody knows, "There's nothing to fear but fear itself." But people with backbone acknowledge that sometimes they are afraid. Afraid of losing something, damaging something, wasting precious time, what have you. To shy away from private fears and proclaim that you don't really have any is decidedly unbackbone-like.

The questions posed here are useful in a variety of business instances: assessing your business, developing new strategies, identifying new opportunities, allocating resources. They can also form the basis for reflecting on your professional priorities. They beget additional questions, so use them as a starting point, and expand in the areas of greatest import to you.

If you can develop Columbo-like questioning capabilities—the competence to understand a situation and choose appropriate questions, the confidence to go to the heart of the matter, and the ability to risk this directness—you'll detect that backbone growing stronger.

BACKBONE-BUILDING EXERCISES

- ### *For Competence*

Pick a puzzling situation, and play Columbo. Come on, get into the role. Imagine that your hair's a little mussed and your shirt's un-tucked. There, now that you're not so worried about how spiffy you look, think about what's going on.

Watch what people are doing, and listen to what they're saying. Scratch your head, Columbo-style, and postulate a bit. Try to understand what's wrong and figure out what questions could help you crack the case.

Give somebody a quizzical Columbo look when you ask a question. See what happens.

- ### *For Confidence*

Assemble the answers you get. What story do they tell? What does that enable you to do?

Ask someone to teach you about something you don't understand but would like to know. This is a favorite Columbo ploy. It sets up a positive exchange of information and often gives you more skinny than you could have asked for.

Remember that every question that crosses your mind doesn't need to exit your mouth. Watch. Listen. Think.

- ### *For Risk Taking*

Imagine a young Columbo; he'd probably have been as direct, but he probably started with little queries. Ask a simple question in a non-threatening situation, such as "What was that deadline, again?"

Direct your questions to specific individuals to improve your chances of getting a meaningful response. Give 'em a Columbo look. Squint your eyes, and study their faces. If you don't get an answer, ask again.

Ask direct and relevant questions, and be brief. Though Columbo appeared to rumble around, when the question flew, it was a dart.

8

Determine the Power Sources

IN EVERY ORGANIZATION, there are those who do and those who talk about doing. Sometimes these are the same people; most times, they're not. By now you've become acquainted with many ways to watch and read what's going on in your organization. You can tell who gets things done and who talks about getting things done. Shirtsleeves do; suits talk. As Goethe admonished, "Create, artist! Do not talk!" Get busy engineering the effectiveness that your organization needs and that you deserve. Build that backbone.

Yes, the art and skill of public speaking is a career asset, and if you have the talent and the inclination to develop this talent, you will have a distinct edge. How-

> People who know little are usually great talkers, while men who know much say little.
>
> ROUSSEAU

ever, nothing substitutes for achievement. Perfect your ability to accomplish things right, well, and consistently, and you'll build a power base that is nearly unassailable.

If you've been around organizations for a while, you're probably pretty good at spotting who the talkers are and who the doers are. You can probably judge with accuracy who really makes things click and who just talks about it. Which of these types are you more impressed by?

Now, before you run off in a whirlwind of determined energy, let's clarify a couple of premises. First, although I'm setting this up as an either-or comparison, it's rarely that definitive. Articulate people are not inherently bad or lazy. Conversely, not all busy people are effective.

Second, great oration has its place. John F. Kennedy fueled the hope and determination of a youthful nation with his famous "Ask not" speech. Martin Luther King Jr. did the same when he roared, "I have a dream." And Eleanor Roosevelt encouraged boldness with her declaration, "No one can make you feel inferior without your consent." Notice, though, that these and many other great speakers were also men and women of action who matched the energy of their words with the ambition of their deeds. People of backbone do, too.

Several years ago, a friend of mine worked for a company that recruited a person with an impressive résumé and a long list of regional public speaking credits. The company relocated this local celebrity and plopped him into the middle of a chaotic division that had been rocked in recent years by change and management turnover.

The speech maker, faced with having to do the very things he gave speeches about, panicked at the stress levels he encountered in the organization. He froze when he had major decisions to make. He tried to do most of the work himself (he had a lot of very good answers, after all) and alienated some very smart and willing helpers in the process. Had the speech maker had a backbone, he'd have called a time-out to reassess where he was and what, realistically, he could do. He'd have recognized that he was a suit trying to be a shirtsleeve.

Why did he take the job in the first place? Why does anyone make a move? To accept a new challenge. To add sparkle to a résumé by virtue of adding a high-profile position with a well-known company. To prove in action what you know in theory. Or try to, anyway.

Beware the traps! As you work to build your backbone, remember that the best suits started out as shirtsleeves. Experience gives depth and believability to their words. Suits that are simply bigger versions of their wordy earlier selves are missing that all-important action part of the equation.

Study the Shirtsleeves to Figure Out How Things Happen

Shirtsleeves don't spend a lot of time jawing about what needs to get done. They're doers. Shirtsleeves have a penchant for action and gain great satisfaction from reviewing their accomplishments at the end of the day. They don't spend a lot of time selling their ideas or their competence; they'd much rather be busy accomplishing. Shirtsleeves like to get others involved in solving problems, allocating appropriate resources to a challenge, and moving forward. They don't like to sit around and debate issues; they're much too focused for that.

Study shirtsleeves. Notice how they make things happen. A lot of them make lists. They prioritize. They channel their energies in pursuit of well-defined goals. They get others engaged, too.

Are these some paragons of corporate perfection? No. But most of them do have backbone. Shirtsleeves with backbone are purposeful and active. They create priorities, keep promises, and deliver the goods. They pay attention in a more intensive and consistent manner than most.

Do they mess up? Sure. Shirtsleeves have bad days and make boneheaded decisions just like the rest of their human brethren. But those with backbone own up to their mistakes. Where they can, they take steps to rectify botched situations. They accept their limitations and don't come unhinged when they discover personal errors.

Shirtsleeves without backbone are the ones who walk around with to-do lists handed to them by someone else, usually the boss. They're busy checking off tasks as quickly as they can, but when a foul-up occurs, they head for the hills, saying, "I just did as I was told."

Let's visit a shirtsleeve with backbone.

Hector is part of the management group of a midsize pharmaceutical distributorship. He and his peers meet weekly to exchange updates on projects, their progress to date, and any problems they're struggling with. There are seven in the group, and each one has responsibility for a functional area of the company. Sales, distribution, information systems, customer service, and three operating divisions are represented.

For one business quarter, I observed Hector and the group, noting the content and manner of each individual's presentation. My responsibility was to provide feedback to each individual and assist in identifying and eliminating roadblocks to progress.

We began the quarter with an outline of specific objectives: incremental increases in sales and on-time shipments, installation of new software to enable faster and more extensive communications, a reduction in customer service complaints, and process and productivity improvements in each of the operating divisions.

For the first few weekly meetings, people gave stream-of-consciousness activity reports about what was going on in their respective areas. Few referred to the goals they had set. Some related specific (and usually unanticipated) problems that had occurred throughout the course of the week and described how they had responded to them. It was evident early on that although they had created an outline of objectives to use as a roadmap, few consulted it. Daily incidents commanded the attention of these managers and demanded continuing reallocation of resources. (It was also evident that most of them were flying by the seat of their pants when it came time for their weekly reports.)

Except for Hector. He showed up each week with summary notes regarding his objectives and how far he had progressed toward achieving them. He, too, related difficulties (it seemed the right thing to do—a commiseration culture predominated), but his descriptions were brief and matter-of-fact. It was as though he were describing yesterday's thunderstorm that temporarily suspended an outdoor picnic. No big deal, just an event that was here and gone, and one that didn't leave any lasting mark.

After a month or so, people began to get uneasy about their lack of progress as they reported on the week's activity. Their reports got shorter and their silences longer. When we went back to the objectives they had set, they became defensive and argumentative. Insufficient resources, they moaned. Not enough time to get everything done. Bad attitudes throughout the company. Quirky clients. Faulty equipment. The litany of complaints about not having the tools or support to get done what they had committed to do grew longer by the week. Tempers flared as tensions rose within the group.

Except for Hector. He didn't bother himself much with the discomforts of the others. He went about his business and told the group each week what had been accomplished. He began to chuckle as he described the innovative work his people were doing, making strides he never knew they were capable of until he told them what he wanted to accomplish by the end of the quarter. They were sharing resources among themselves, changing the way little things got done, and each week coming to him with greater enthusiasm and energy as they cataloged their successes. Few of the weekly accomplishments amounted to anything noteworthy on their own, but together and over time, they represented steady advances toward the achievement of the quarterly objectives.

Hector's unassuming manner had fooled many. Had we taken a vote, he'd have been elected least likely of the management group to deliver the goods on his projects. Why? Because he wasn't a promoter, he wasn't familiar with the latest management fads, and when he spoke, his comments were brief and to the point.

Hector is a shirtsleeve.

Many of the others are suits. They like to analyze their approaches to their people and to prioritizing work. They prefer to discuss challenges rather than tackle them. They worry aloud about best practices and whether or not they are in tune with them. Meanwhile, they do little— no sense rushing headlong into battle if they're not convinced they have the best method in mind.

During our time together, they contemplated the order in which work should be done, taking care to understand how task A might impinge upon task B. (Their Gantt charts and milestones were meticulously detailed and reviewed; action had not as yet been initiated.) They railed about late or inaccurate reports and how these impeded their decision-making efforts. (Bad data fields, confusing formats, and other minutiae consumed their attention.) They delineated who should be recognized for what, and in what manner. (Incentive and recognition programs are vital to good employee morale.) They considered whose feelings might be hurt if they were not tended to at a moment of personal crisis. (Responsiveness and compassion are cornerstones of enlightened management.)

The suits talked; the shirtsleeve did. Who do you suppose wielded the power and influence anytime a new initiative was proposed? For that matter, who do you suppose got the nod more often than not for piloting new initiatives? Right. Hector.

Contrast Hector with Doug. Doug is a marketing manager for a sales promotion agency in the Midwest. Doug's a promoter. He fancies himself the Alfred E. Newman type, quick with a quip and light on his feet. Doug is not just a suit; he's an empty suit. Every morning, he bounds through his department, spewing buzzwords and bragging about the big-name client on whom he's calling later in the morning. (At one point, he was talking about doing a deal with Lassie.)

Doug is a hilarious guy. But he never actually sells the deal, never actually signs the big-name client, and never actually makes the big killing that will send him in glory to his yacht to sail off into a golden sunset, ripe with success.

Doug loves to talk, but he knows not how to do. And he has every known reason why things just don't quite seem to click. That big-name client? A moron. Lassie? Sick. His sure-to-strike-it-rich business plan? Still in development. Poor Doug. He needs a backbone.

From a distance, the Dougs of the world look like shirtsleeves because they move around a lot. But you have to check results before you can bestow the shirtsleeves honor.

As you build your own campaign for greater power and influence, take special note of who in your organization consistently gets results. Study these people. Talk to them to find out how they operate. Contrast what they do with the actions of others who are less successful in making things happen.

Intimidation Techniques and Why They're Short-Term

How many times have you heard comments like this: "That's a great idea, but you don't know the company; it doesn't work like that here." "Maybe that was true for someone else, but you don't know Sharon." "I'd like to think there was some merit in that suggestion, but it's clear you don't have the background to fully understand what you're suggesting." And a premier putdown, "Where did you come up with that scheme?"

Anywhere you find power, you'll find power struggles and intimidation techniques. Suits such as Doug like to intimidate shirtsleeves in order to slow them down; if they can be stymied even a little, the other's nonproductivity won't be so obvious. Doug likes to borrow buzzwords from M.B.A. programs and technologists to hurl at shirtsleeves. He likes to see the confusion on their faces—he feels as if he's shown them who's the smarter. And shirtsleeves with backbone do stop. The first time or two. They look at Doug as if he's a little mad and they're not quite sure what to make of his blather. But a couple of times like that, and they've got his number. Then they just keep doing what they were doing, knowing that Doug will continue to trip the light fantastic to Lord knows what end.

People with real power—shirtsleeves with backbone who get things done—have no need to intimidate, and they don't succumb to intimidation techniques. They feel the pangs, certainly. Anytime someone openly challenges you or tries to make you look foolish, you feel awkward and uncertain. But they manage these reactions and stand firm in the face of idle threat.

"You don't know what you're talking about," and "That won't work here" are "killer phrases," according to creativity expert Chic Thompson. Killer phrases are used mostly out of habit, he says, and it's up to anyone who hears them to put a stop to them. He suggests getting the offender's attention quickly—throw a Nerf ball or a wad of paper—and challenging the mental laziness that prompts the killer phrase.

It's great advice. But few people follow it. Who, after all, is going to come back at someone who has just put him or her down? People with backbone, that's who.

Comments like "That's a great idea, but it won't work here" are not benign. While many people prefer to shrug them off as bad habits and not anything to get worked up about, you can see that they shut down input, end discussion, and prevent true exploration.

Melanie met this particular intimidation technique as she was presenting a new marketing plan to senior management. She wanted to incorporate a new supplier into her stable of providers and use the new services available from this source to enhance a key client program. Her plan to do so was the subject of her presentation to management.

Mike, head of production, stopped her cold. "You have no idea what you're talking about. You came in here with your highfalutin' ideas three years ago, and not one of them has had anything to do with what we do here." (But every one of them has resulted in new business.)

Melanie was taken aback and shocked into silence. Mike continued his tirade for another minute or two, while the other senior managers watched Melanie. She let silence settle in while she gathered her thoughts. She looked for a long moment at Mike. Then she resumed her presentation by taking a step back and describing the market conditions for her client, the new services offered by the supplier, and why the two created not only a perfect match but also a golden opportunity for the company to take a bold leadership step on her client's behalf. Melanie's backbone made Mike's challenge look silly.

Had Melanie been less clear about her purpose going into the meeting, she might have been cowed into confusion. Had she been less certain of how the supplier could meet an as-yet-untapped need, she might have second-guessed herself into defeat. But she knew exactly what she wanted to accomplish, and she quietly stood her ground.

There are times, though, when an attack like Mike's catches you unprepared. At moments like these, when somebody tries to shut you down by telling you that for some reason you don't get it, consider conceding the point. Engage your backbone to admit that you don't know the specifics of what your challenger asserts. Allow that perhaps you don't fully understand the complexity of the problem. Ask questions that will help clarify your understanding. Take notes on what is said following intimidating and dismissive remarks. Listen. Postulate how you can help solve the problem without driving people further into their positions.

How is this a demonstration of backbone? By furthering your understanding of both the situation and the person involved, you're building competence. What your challenger says in response to your request for more information will tell you much about how smart or self-assured he or she is. By acknowledging your knowledge deficiency—an unthinkable risk for the backboneless—you refuse to accept the intimidation aimed at you. This is an act of confidence that will surprise many. Their view of you will sharpen instantly, and their high-horse routines will eventually cease.

Some intimidation tactics are subtle and may be hard to interpret. Little hijackings fall into this category. Hijackings occur when someone usurps power by changing the subject, diverting attention and energy, or creating unnecessary crises. Little hijackings rattle weak backbones.

Jack is the manager of corporate communications in a midsize, privately held professional services firm. He was asked by the president to lead a meeting of senior managers to prioritize a long list of issues that had been hotly debated but largely unresolved for the past three years. Jack's task was to succinctly outline the issues in agenda form, facilitate a brief discussion of each one, and lead the group in an exercise to select two or three of them for priority action within the next six to nine months.

Each of the other managers had been assigned a topic to summarize. They were to present a synopsis of previous discussion and research on their topic and recap any recommendations that had been made in prior discussions.

Jack had begun the meeting and reached a point of explaining the method they would use to determine their priorities when one of the most senior members of the group joined them. He made his way quickly to a chair and waited impatiently for a break in the discussion. When a brief pause presented itself, the senior manager broke into the meeting abruptly.

"Jack, what's going on with the Davidson account? I just got word that there's a problem with production and we're not going to make our ship date. What's the deal?"

Uh-oh. Here comes the hijack.

Jack, taken by surprise in front of the president and his management peers, looked at his attacker a little stupidly. He fumbled to gather his thoughts and made a vague remark about having to look into the situation more closely before being able to respond.

"What are you doing here?" demanded his attacker. "Shouldn't you be working on that instead?"

Another manager, a friend of Jack's, jumped to his aid. "Actually, I heard that things are pretty much under control at the moment."

> He's a wonderful talker, who has the art of telling you nothing in a great harangue.
>
> MOLIÈRE

"Since when?" shouted the senior manager, in a growing state of frenzy. "I talked to Bob (the salesman) twenty minutes ago, and he was furious. He said the client is having a fit and he's getting no response from anyone here."

Now Jack's got big trouble. The president's eyebrows have gone up, and he's leaning over the table in Jack's direction. Several other managers have cast their eyes to the floor; they hate to watch people get grilled. The senior manager who hijacked the meeting is glaring at Jack and pressuring him for a solution.

Two other managers who have not completed their assignments for this meeting are happy at the prospect of having it postponed. They chime in with bits of hearsay information from production managers and the salesman about the Davidson problem. They want to keep the conversation centered on this digression for as long as they can.

Predictably, the meeting in session was suspended. Jack was admonished by the senior manager to find a quick solution to the Davidson problem and to give a full accounting of the situation to the president when he had finished. Humiliated and angry at having been hijacked in such a way, Jack marched, stiff-legged, from the meeting.

The others drifted out, glad to have the extra time to do whatever called for their attention. The long-standing issues were left unprioritized and unresolved yet again.

Similar scenes take place routinely in many organizations today. Priorities get scrambled in the face of new panic, and bad behavior is excused in the name of expedient customer service.

But with backbone, you can refuse to be intimidated. When someone is aggressively negative in his or her approach to you, speak softly. If the person is agitated, don't try to intervene or make a point. Let the steam blow. Your interest is in producing, not arguing. Politely acknowledge the challenge, and make note of it. Then return to the work at hand until you can wrap it up to your satisfaction. Will this be easy? No way. Will it feel comfortable? Of course not. In fact, it will feel scary more often than not. Will it set you apart as someone with backbone who knows how to stay on track and get things done? Absolutely.

If Jack had had a backbone, he'd have excused himself briefly and called one of his employees to ask that immediate attention be given to the Davidson problem. He'd have asked for an update on the situation within thirty minutes. That done, he'd have returned to the meeting in session and the management imperatives, per plan.

In the heat of the moment, Jack clearly did not exert backbone. Habit, culture, and his fear of having lost control kept him doing what's always been done in a hijacking situation. And a lack of backbone is what keeps this company spinning its wheels.

Jack's challenger is a bully, and bullies are great fans of intimidation techniques. Many run over others for the sheer fun of watching people dive for cover. Rarely do bullies get down to productive problem solving; they prefer, instead, to demonstrate whatever power they think they have through fabricated or one-sided skirmishes. You'll often find bullies in the middle of disrupted programs and confused and scared workers. They like to stand tall while others quake.

Strong ego insecurity makes bullies act tough, but it also makes them fairly easy to counter. They have no backbone, so they're readily confused when you stand up to them. When you find yourself in the crosshairs of a bully's attack rifle, don't waver from the business problem at hand. Use questions to clarify the reason for the ire. Make the antagonist tell you specifically what he or she is unhappy about. Refuse to respond to personal attacks or petty criticisms. Remember, sticks and stones might break your bones, but the bully still has the problem. When bullies meet backbones, intimidation techniques are short-lived.

Why Silence Is Golden

When intimidators arrive on the scene, silence is sometimes your very best friend. Isaac Babel said it so well: "No steel can pierce the human heart so chillingly as a period at the right moment."

When you hold your tongue, some attackers skid to a stop. They wonder what's going on. They look around for supporters. The act of holding your tongue is a declaration of backbone that turns intimidation back on the intimidator and sends the weakest ones scurrying off, tail between their legs.

Some intimidators are more tenacious. They'll continue badgering you in the hope of drawing you into a fight. They know how easy it is for people with weak backbones to be lured into arguments. They've seen babbling of all sorts break out when people are nervous or scared or otherwise set aflutter by their tactics. Every time this happens, intimidators draw satisfaction and strength to continue their browbeating ways. People with backbone understand the power of silence to discourage intimidators and to declare their refusal to be threatened.

People with backbone also understand that intimidators will try to cast their silence as weakness or martyrdom. Downcast eyes and slumped shoulders invite this renewed attack. Be watchful of how you use silence and what you say with your face and body when you hold your tongue. Direct eye contact, a little smile, or a slight shrug of the shoulders says, "I understand what you're trying to do, and I'm not playing the game."

David had to learn this lesson in the school of hard knocks. He was a project manager working on a team with high-power, big-ego colleagues. The grandest of these was Rick, a supremely aggressive sales guy who had little time for weak people or lame excuses. Rick, by the way, was a bully. He strutted and fumed and otherwise made big productions out of little developments that others handled as a matter of course. Rick had a significant stake in letting the team know who was in charge.

In one particularly tense meeting, David was running through project tasks and deadlines, showing where the two met happily and where there were gaps. Three of six deadlines were in jeopardy, and Rick was livid.

Screaming about his credibility with the client, Rick demanded to know why David had let things slide so horrendously. He demanded to know, too, how David could have any pride in his work as a project "manager." What kind of management did David think he was providing?

David was stunned into a stupified silence. This sent Rick over the reasonableness edge, and he lit into David with a vengeance. He challenged David's competence, his ability to get others to keep their commitments to deadlines, and his dedication to the team. When he got tired of beating on David, Rick charged from the meeting to find David's boss.

Fortunately, David's boss had both a backbone and Rick's number, as well as mine! He calmed Rick and put David to work with me. Our mission: to help David become more effective through the development of a stronger backbone. (No, we didn't call it this, but it's certainly what we did.)

David learned to take a longer view of situations in order to fortify himself when Rick erupted. He studied the team's big-picture obligations to the client and the company, which helped him put Rick's demands in perspective. He learned to remind Rick of things done well when Rick found nothing but petty fault. He learned to choose specific times to remain silent and how to do so with strength and patience rather than in an attitude of submission. He became adept at giving Rick a raised eyebrow or a wry smile when Rick threatened a rant. David grew an impressive backbone and learned to use silence as an extremely effective intimidation deflector.

Silence serves another very useful backbone purpose. When you reflect in silence upon something said, you convey an image of intelligent interest. You also grease the skids of dialogue. As Sydney Smith, an eighteenth-century writer, once said of a contemporary, "He has occasional flashes of silence that make his conversation perfectly delightful."

When Yes Really Means No . . . or Maybe

When it's your turn to make things happen at work, it's important to understand ways in which power gets diverted and energy dissipated.

False starts are a leading cause of power disruption and meandering effort.

Group meetings that drag on for hours are spawning grounds for aborted attempts and unreliable commitments. So are situations in which ideas are presented with great enthusiasm and a request for a speedy yes or no answer. Many executives in these instances offer tentative agreement because they like the presenters' energy and initiative. If this provisional aspect of the agreement is emphasized, a later reversal is generally accepted with grace. Too often, though, enthusiastic idea people take quick assent at face value and begin at once to round up the resources necessary for implementation.

These people often view themselves as can-do shirtsleeves: the movers and shakers of their organizations, always willing to take swift and determined action. When their ideas get deep-sixed after they thought they'd been approved, their disappointment is keen.

To understand the true power sources at work, you have to recognize when "yes" really means "no" or, at best, "maybe."

People who lack backbone often run with a new-idea ball and then stew when their project later gets sidelined. They whine about wishy-washy management and wonder aloud why it's always their work that gets scrapped.

People with backbone pay attention to what's going on at the point of decision and project approval. They watch for reality checks like fidgety body language, signs of fatigue or distraction, and wavering eye contact. All of these traits signal less than optimal attention, and where attention wanes, subpar understanding is predictable. So is capricious commitment. These are all common toward the end of a long meeting.

Where a new idea rushes in on a wave of super energy, watch for wide-open eyes, nodding heads, and enthusiastic but shallow smiles and remarks. These all indicate appreciation for the presentation. But be careful not to translate presentation appreciation into project approval.

To be sure that the "yes" they heard is what it is, people with backbone summarize their request and verify the approval. They often get it in writing, even if it's only in the form of a short note or an E-mail message from the head of a committee. Most people are reluctant to do this, because it opens the door for a reversal of a positive decision. But fooling yourself by running with an approval that you know in your gut to be tentative is irresponsible. And claiming unfair or biased treatment when the plug is pulled is silly. Wasteful, too. And a tip-off that your backbone needs fortification.

How to Tap Power Sources

Once you've identified who the shirtsleeves are in your organization, befriend them. Call on them for advice. Ask them to challenge your ideas and assumptions. In Chapter 6 we talked about associations. Shirtsleeves tend to hang together, so tap the network.

If appropriate, offer to assist them on projects, proofread reports, or play devil's advocate to a favorite project of theirs. Share news of interest to them. Watch for the little touches that make these people so proficient: an extra two minutes of conversation with someone from whom they need help, quick notes jotted as they walk down the hall, extensive phone and face-to-face communication, an attitude of personal responsibility for making good things happen. Adopt these habits as your own. In short, demonstrate that you, too, are interested in advancing the aims of the organization by working smarter with winning style.

But be genuine. You can just imagine our empty-suit friend Doug horning in on shirtsleeves' action, trying to ingratiate himself by teaching them the latest buzzwords. People with backbone won't have it. So, take time to develop your power base. Show genuine interest in other shirtsleeves, and put yourself in a position of sharing your best expertise. Mutual respect is what you're after. When you need support for your own work, ask for it directly from these people. Avoid the ones who stand in the limelight at every opportunity. While they may be able to help you gain visibility for your project, they are also likely to try to steal your thunder.

Shirtsleeves with backbone—the real power sources of any organization—can help you in concrete and reliable ways. For maximum backbone effectiveness, associate regularly with them.

BACKBONE-BUILDING EXERCISES

- ### *For Competence*

Sort the suits and the shirtsleeves in your organization, and watch what they do. Each wields power; you want the kind that can be counted on to get to the finish line.

Inspect intimidation techniques. (From a distance, if you can.) See how people who want power but don't have it use dominance tactics to pretend they're in charge. Note the lackluster results.

Practice silence. Examine what develops in the noise void.

- ### *For Confidence*

Get busy! Talk less about what you're going to do; just go do it.

Keep track of what you get done over the next three weeks. Compare the number and scope of successful completions from week one to week three. Is there a noticeable difference?

Figure out when a "yes" is really a "yes" and when it's something else. Act on reality, not on wishful projection.

- ### *For Risk Taking*

If you've been a timid doer, crank up your energy and output. Don't worry about telling other people how terrific you are—show 'em.

Face down a bully. Just look; don't say a word. Shrug, grin, and get back to work. The bully will soon shop for fun elsewhere.

Solidify tacit approval by getting a solid commitment. If your project gets the great-idea-but-not-a-priority-right-now decision, set it aside to work on live projects. You want to channel and direct power, not waste it.

9

Lose the Excuses

Do YOU WANT to be regarded as someone important, influential, and trustworthy? If so, lose the excuses. All of them. Now.

Anytime you provide an excuse, regardless of its veracity, you demonstrate to others that you are unwilling to take responsibility for something that was entrusted to you. It's hard to imagine never using excuses again. Maybe it's an impossible goal. But if you want to be held out as someone special, someone worth paying attention to because success is written all over you, lose the excuses.

You might be tempted to argue that there are times when excuses are valid explanations for why something did or didn't happen as planned. There *are* times when an explanation is appropriate and welcome, but they are rare, and

> **While you're saving your face, you're losing your ass.**
>
> PRESIDENT LYNDON JOHNSON

because so many people offer up excuses in lieu of results, credible reasons are often misjudged as excuses. When does a valid explanation become an excuse? When it's offered after a problem has progressed to a stage where fixing it has become impossible.

I have made a commitment to provide notes to a department secretary by noon Tuesday so she can have a complete report prepared for a board meeting Wednesday morning. The notes will detail the current quarter's business results for my area of the company, and they're integral to the overall operations picture. On Friday of the week before my notes are due, I schedule a client meeting for Tuesday morning. I realize as I'm scheduling the meeting that this may preclude me from providing the notes on time for inclusion in Wednesday's report.

Now I have a dilemma. The client meeting is important—several new programs are up for renewal, and my presence could speed the client's decision to renew. But the notes are important, too. I consider calling the secretary in charge of assembling the final report, sharing my dilemma, and asking for her help in finding a solution. I veto this idea, deciding instead to work on my notes over the weekend and get them to her before the original deadline. I don't want to let her down, but I also don't want to call attention to the fact that I've overcommitted myself.

Predictably, the weekend flies by and I don't get to the notes. No problem: I still have a few open time slots on Monday, and if all else fails, I'll stay up as late as I need to on Monday night to make sure the notes get done. All time evaporates on Monday, my teenage daughter needs help with a last-minute project on Monday evening (where did she learn to procrastinate so?), and by midnight I'm a wreck. Thinking I'd better get some sleep before the heap-big client meeting on Tuesday, I fall into bed and sleep fitfully.

At 9:00 Tuesday morning, the secretary calls to remind me that my notes are due by noon. I apologize profusely and tell her I will not be able to provide them. I point out that in fact I'm on my way out the door in ten minutes for an important client meeting that will likely result in new business for the company.

I hang up the phone and leave the building feeling awful. The secretary is upset, the report is incomplete, and I have no good explanation for my failure to meet my commitment.

I intended to. I really did! I just ran out of time. But I'm tending instead to important company business—more important business, in fact, than writing up a bunch of notes.

Sound familiar?

We all make excuses. And by the time we're dragging them out, we're usually feeling guilty or deficient or just plain bad. We're definitely feeling defensive.

Making excuses is a poor waste of everyone's time and energy. It also destroys our credibility and trustworthiness more quickly than any other single act. And it's most unbackbone-like.

What might have changed both the outcome and the tenor of the foregoing example? The Friday phone call to the secretary that I decided against. Had I made that call, we might have talked about who else could have completed the notes. I could have delegated the job to someone in the division and then reviewed them before they were submitted for the final report. I could have relieved the self-imposed pressure on my weekend and felt more patience toward my teenage daughter. In the end, I could have been viewed as a valuable and busy executive who kept my word and took care of even "small" projects in the course of doing my job.

Whining: The Ultimate Suicide

Whining is a close cousin to excuse making, but it's even more annoying. Whining is the practice of complaining about all things that make one's life difficult. Whining includes complaints about the weather, one's health, one's family members, pets, and possessions. Whining includes bemoaning global warming, static cling, hair loss, memory loss, lost love, and lost opportunity. Whining is a pathetic announcement that the whiner is a loser. Whining is the ultimate suicide. In a business world that demands the attention, energy, and concentration of every worker worth the job he or she holds, there is no place for whining.

Listed here are some classic excuses that echo down corporate hallways every day of the workweek. They qualify as examples of whining because they are facts of business life to which qualified and mature professionals (people with backbone) adapt.

- She won't listen/understand . . .
- He'll get upset . . .
- I'll lose my job . . .
- Nothing ever changes . . .
- I don't know if it will/can work . . .
- I don't have the support/resources I need . . .
- She's mad at me . . .
- He'll go ballistic as he always does when something surprises him . . .
- He won't do anything about it . . .
- I don't have time . . .
- I have to do X, Y, and Z first . . .
- She didn't get stuff to me on time . . .

- He forgot to call me back . . .
- I don't know where things stand . . .
- She's still thinking about it . . .

At the end of each of these complaints (which may represent a true statement—she probably *won't* listen) comes silence and a defeated sense of resignation. There is no effort at finding another way to express something, to do something different, or to accept responsibility for creating the situation that has become problematic.

People with backbone look at these and other typical obstacles and figure out a way to succeed despite them. Let's go through the list.

"She won't listen or understand" becomes "In the past, she hasn't listened when I've presented things in this way. Maybe if I rearrange my presentation or start off with something I know is important to her, she'll respond differently." It would not be unusual for this nonwhiner to seek assistance from coworkers or friends who have experience at making persuasive presentations.

"He'll get upset" is not an excuse to people with backbone. It is an acknowledged fact that is considered carefully and investigated for the reasons behind the reaction. (This is where attention paid to those discovery areas that we discussed in Chapter 2 pays off.) With some clues about what causes the other person to become upset, the person with backbone will seek an opportunity to talk to him about the situation. People without backbone won't dare "approach the lion's den."

"I'll lose my job" may sound extreme, but for many workers in our downsizing, rightsizing, merging, acquiring, and restructuring business circus, this is a real concern. However, keep in mind that companies need people who will take time to scope out a situation, come up with alternative approaches, weigh larger implications of these alternatives, troubleshoot, and brainstorm solutions to potential problems relating to alternatives.

People who are able to do these things—and who take the risk—are people who win. Sometimes suggestions are uncomfortable and may even seem outrageous on the surface. But when suggestions are born of knowledge of the company and attention to its unique challenges, and when these suggestions are thought through from implementation to result, it's difficult to undermine their appropriateness. It's difficult, too, to view the people who offer them as termination targets.

On the other hand, if you routinely use several of the phrases we're discussing here, you probably will lose your job at some point.

"Nothing ever changes" is a defeatist cop-out. What, specifically do you want to change? What would need to happen to initiate this change? Who needs to be involved? What is the driver for these people? Can you show them that by helping you create change, they will realize some of their goals, too? The old saw (which every change expert so irritatingly invokes) is true: "If you are not part of the solution, you are part of the problem." A corollary might be: "If you can't figure out which is which, you are in serious trouble."

"I don't know if it will/can work" is a valid statement. No one knows until things are tried. Whiners say these words and move on to something else. People with backbone know that if you try something and it doesn't work, you scratch it off your idea list. If you try something and it does work, you present your experiment, ask for additional resources, and put effort behind expanding the success. Notice I didn't say go public first. When you try new things, it's wise to try them on a small scale, using limited resources. Don't promise the next great revelation of something before you know what you've got. The people who like this excuse have usually failed at something in the past and have become too gun-shy to try again. They quit before they start. These people need to grow some backbone.

"I don't have the support/resources I need" gives whiners the excuse they seek to stop working on a project or an idea. To people with backbone, it becomes a challenge. "If I truly want to accomplish this, I need to describe what I need, why I need it, for how long I expect to use it, and what I expect to produce at the end." Wow, that's a lot of work! No wonder so many people just whine.

"She's mad at me" stops whiners in their tracks. For people with backbone, it's a relatively unimportant observation. Mood problems don't stop strong people from working on high-priority ideas or projects. If someone's mood prevents her from engaging in a meaningful business discussion, the person with backbone will come back another day or take the discussion to someone who is not in a funk. When we learn to accept people's quirks matter-of-factly and persist in our efforts for the good of the business, we find we're better able to work with all sorts of funny people.

"He'll go ballistic as he always does when something surprises him" is a no-brainer. The important part of that complaint is "when something surprises him." Knowing this helps you in your dealings with the person. Don't surprise him! Tell him what's going on, why you're doing what you're doing, what you hope to accomplish or gain when you're finished, and how he can support your effort. In a business environment, no one likes to be surprised. There are too many demands we know about that drain our attention and energy; dropping something new into the mix is inviting an outburst.

"He won't do anything about it" is another excuse to immobilize your-self. What, specifically, do you want him to do? Figure this out, and then ask him to do it. When you take a vague complaint to someone in charge, it likely *will* be ignored if you don't also present an idea to address it. Why? Because if you have not taken the time to try to understand the problem about which you're complaining, and you haven't given any thought to how it might be settled, why should someone who is not suf-fering from the problem take time away from his own problems to fix yours? If I can't get the copy machine to work properly, and I haven't asked someone to help me, and I haven't called the repair guy, but I'm having a fit because I need to get a report done, who is going to rush to my assistance?

By the way, if you think that was a silly example, believe me when I tell you that I see this very instance happen time and time again. Usu-ally it's "important" people who don't have time to mess around with such trifles as unjamming copy machines or dealing directly with the people who do. But they sure get stuck because of it.

"I don't have time" is the primo loser excuse. If you don't have time, why did you say you'd do it? No one else rules your time, and no one else commits it for you unless you give them the permission and power. Let's be clear: "I don't have time" qualifies as an excuse only after you've agreed to do something and then realize you can't. When you say it *before* you commit to something, you're stating a *reason* for not taking on the addi-tional activity. But when you say you will and then you don't, "I don't have time" is a poor excuse, and you know it. The people on the receiv-ing end are justified in feeling acute disappointment and even scorn.

"I have to do X, Y, and Z first" is similar to the no-time defense. While some folks may be interested to know everything on your to-do list, chances are that most people don't care. What they want to know is whether or not you can participate with them in some project. If you can, say so and make a personal commitment to follow through. If you can't, say so and let it go.

Too often, you say you will help even when you know that your time is limited and your contribution is likely to be minimal. You commit because you want others to think of you as a "player." You want to be in the middle of things because it makes you feel important. But nothing erodes that importance and your reputation as a player faster than saying "yes" and behaving "no." Worse, when you say yes and continually turn people away with the excuse that you have so many other things to do first, you tell them their projects are not important enough to rearrange your priorities in order to keep your commitments. You also tell them you are ineffective at managing your own life.

"She didn't get stuff to me on time" may, once again, be a true statement. But it has little to do with your own performance of a task. You surely were aware that you needed input from someone else to complete your work. It is up to you to get what you need or to adjust your commitments when you see a problem develop. To fail in your delivery and point backward to someone else is weak, ineffective, and, over time, suicidal. It screams "no backbone."

"He forgot to call me back." Ditto.

"I don't know where things stand" is an admission that you lack information. It is not a reason to blow someone off and go back to doing something else. If you are asked a question about a project in which you have responsibility, "I don't know where things stand" is acceptable as a temporary state only when you act quickly to find out. You wouldn't think of saying "I don't know" to your boss and leaving it at that. Don't do so with others who depend on you.

"She's still thinking about it" feels shallow when you say it, doesn't it? When someone asks you about a resolution, a decision, or an action to be taken and you point to someone else, you confess your inability to deliver. You admit your powerlessness, and you relinquish whatever status you might have had. Call her instead. Ask her what her thoughts are, where her problem areas lie, and what you might do to provide additional information so that a decision can be reached. This is backbone in action.

When it comes to speaking up, there's a whole laundry list of reasons why people who lack backbone can't do it. As you know, these are excuses to lose. Here's a sampling. The real reasons for the excuses are shown in parentheses.

I can't say that because:

- It's not my place (I'm lazy or scared).
- It's not my job (I'm lazy).
- I won't be heard (I have no credibility with the group).
- I'm uncertain of my message or the response I'll get (I'm scared).
- They don't pay me enough (I'm angry).
- I'm not sure I should know this. I don't know how much I should know, how much I should learn, how much I should do. (I'm confused.) *Who will tell me what to do?*

Whenever you're afraid to speak up, take time to figure out what's going on with you. If you are simply uncertain about how to present something, seek help from your associates or from a friend who is good with words. Review the big-picture map you created in Chapter 1. Go back to the discovery sessions outlined in Chapter 2, and start attending them again. Pull out your notes on the subject. Factor in your assessments of the people involved. Arrange your thoughts in a larger context to help you gain confidence in their validity and importance.

If you're afraid of irritating someone, be steadfast in your focus on the business project or problem. Personalities do get in the way when you allow them to, and they prevent many good ideas from ever seeing the light of day. Don't let that happen to you. Buck up, figure out what is important about what you think, and present it. Ask someone to help you prepare. If it helps you take the first step toward speaking up, ask someone to go with you when you present your idea.

Why Betrayal Doesn't Hurt

If you've spent any time at all in business, you've probably been exposed to situations in which an associate took advantage of you. Maybe someone used information you relayed in confidence to expose a weakness of yours. Maybe someone promised to support you on a project and turned tail when it met with disapproval at higher levels. Maybe someone you thought was a friend turned out to be a conniving competitor. In these and many other like situations, it hurts to be surprised and betrayed by someone you trusted. You feel disappointment, anger, even shock sometimes. But if you have a strong and resilient backbone, you can glide past these feelings and end up better off for the experience.

Sounds Pollyannaish, you say? Let's explore a couple of examples.

Kurt, a junior-level executive, spent six months working with Chuck, a senior-level mentor who was not his boss. Together, the two men created a brand-new program concept designed to win substantial new business for their firm. As they researched their concept, they found it necessary to include one other executive in their discussions because of his expertise. In addition, Kurt was required to provide general summaries of his work to his boss to justify the time spent away from normal job duties. This requirement was not particularly stringent because the bulk of the new-concept work was done before or after normal business hours.

Kurt worked long hours tracking down information, testing initial concepts, and detailing the project in careful notes. He didn't mind that Chuck didn't share in the footwork; he was grateful for the wisdom and guidance the older man provided. Kurt learned a great

> **An empty bag cannot stand upright.**
> POOR RICHARD'S ALMANAC

deal about how top-level managers think, how they choose projects to support with precious corporate resources, and how to separate relevant information from other interesting but tangential facts.

When it came time to present the new concept to an in-house "board of directors," Kurt was squeezed out. The executive with specialized expertise was called on to assist the senior executive in making the presentation. Kurt was stunned. He couldn't believe that Chuck would betray his hard work, his dedication, and his loyalty not only to the project but also to him. Kurt went to his boss for advice on how to reclaim his position on the project or at the very least to get the credit he deserved for its success.

Kurt's boss smiled a sad, slow smile and advised the junior executive to roll with the punches. He told him to consider himself fortunate for having had the experience, to follow up with his mentor to see how he could now help with project implementation, and to try to understand why he was excluded at the last minute. He talked about power, about how it is used, shared, and granted to others. He explained that while Kurt played a vital role in the project's creation and documentation, his youth and inexperience could prove to be liabilities in an intense, challenging meeting with top-level decision makers. The wise boss further advised the junior executive to store his hurt and angry feelings in a place for recollection at a time when he might be sorely tempted to pull a similar stunt with someone less powerful than he.

This is a tough situation for anyone to negotiate gracefully. Few who have experienced something similar have had the benefit of a wise and stable boss to help them through it. In a competitive, fast-moving business environment, these kinds of things happen all the time. Whether they should or shouldn't is immaterial. People with backbone will learn, grow, and become stronger as a result of the experience. They *will* appreciate the learning. They will become smarter, savvier, and more adept in ticklish situations. They will allocate their time judiciously in the future and will seek opportunities for further learning, regardless of where the credit goes when the day is done. People with backbone will not label this as a betrayal. They will label it as a profitable learning experience.

People without backbone, on the other hand, will whine about how they were used and discarded. They'll resent the time and energy they spent only to have some big shot bask in the glow of undeserved success. They'll waste even more time, energy, and attention feeling awful about something now past, instead of applying lessons learned. People without a backbone will label this as betrayal and will allow themselves to be stymied by it.

In another example, two young women were vying for a promotion. Both were qualified, although their skills and experiences differed. One woman was particularly adept at interpersonal transactions; the other woman had a strong command of is and finance but fewer people skills. The women knew they were each being considered for the promotion. In fact, they had discussed how they could support and help each other regardless of who got the new job. Over several weeks, they each worked diligently at their respective jobs, knowing that strong performance in their current roles was a prerequisite for advancement.

In addition to this conscientious work, the woman with the strong interpersonal skills began to visit with people in the finance and is areas of the company to understand their needs and their unique contributions to the success of the firm. She explored special areas of conflict and brainstormed potential solutions. She made no promises to these associates, nor did she do anything to discredit her "opponent."

This investigative work earned the woman special favor with both the is and finance groups because she asked them directly about their work and concerns. The other woman, being skilled in both these areas, appeared to assume that she knew what they wanted and needed. This disappointed and irritated some.

Perhaps predictably, the woman who did her homework won the promotion. While she was less knowledgeable about business in general, she had demonstrated her willingness to learn. She had further demonstrated her ability to work with others to get at specific and real issues instead of being content to work on generalities or assumptions. Of the two, she had the stronger claim to characteristics required of leaders.

Her opponent, on learning that she had been "passed over" for the promotion, complained bitterly to friends about how the other woman had betrayed her. She said the company had made a stupid mistake, but she was glad to know how appointments here were made—by schmoozing rather than through the demonstration of knowledge. She left the company in short order.

Isn't it interesting that some people choose to pull out the betrayal card as an excuse for not getting something they wanted when, in fact, they had the same opportunity others did? This is weak behavior, and it's repulsive to others. When you begin to build backbone, you take responsibility for what you want, you figure out ways to get it credibly, you do the homework necessary, and you accept the outcome with grace, knowing you did the best you could. You don't turn situational defeat into a further excuse to become a whiner or a slacker. Rather, you invest the time to understand, learn, and grow. Companies love these growth-oriented people.

If You Can't, Someone Else Can

Make no mistake about this. If you decide, for whatever reason (no time, too much else to do, not sure of yourself, too good for that kind of work), that you can't do something, there are probably ten people lined up who can. Some of them will be less experienced and less sophisticated than you, so you probably won't worry much when they get the call to undertake something you consider trivial. But watch out. These candidates will continue to accomplish the little things, and before you know it, they will have reputations as trustworthy, do-anything workers. When the bigger, more challenging projects arise, you may or may not get the call. That depends on your own track record and your willingness to participate in a variety of projects, working with a wide range of people.

When you stop getting the little calls, you better take action. It won't be long before the big calls will cease, too.

A friend of mine learned this lesson the embarrassing way. For a time, she was one of the trustworthy, do-anything workers. Then she got some wayward advice from a book that told her she was "too good to do the grunt work" and she would be wise to set herself above and beyond those kinds of jobs to "create an image as a seasoned and savvy professional." She took the words to heart, and even though she felt a little awkward, she began cultivating relationships with people of greater stature than herself and turning away from the more lowly work she had previously done without protest.

She began handing off trivial projects, explaining to those to whom she gave them that they needed to learn how to perform these assignments if they were to realize their aspirations of advancement up the executive ranks. On the surface, there's nothing wrong with this advice. But she didn't follow it herself. Besides that, she developed the bad habit of stepping to the front of the take-credit line when projects were completed well (but not by her).

As lower-level workers gained competence and confidence, my friend found herself aced out of higher-level projects. It seemed that no one wanted to team up with a person who liked to hand off work but stand up for credit. And the once "lesser" workers who had grown professionally by accepting her project handoffs were suddenly more skilled. They had already proved themselves to be more trustworthy.

My friend was embarrassed and upset at having been overtaken in this way, but to her credit, she was able to retrace her steps to understand that she was the creator of her own temporary demise. She vowed to get busy rectifying her situation before she became truly dispensable.

Remember this story the next time you are tempted to say no to something you have the time, expertise, and energy to do but would simply rather not. Your willingness to do whatever it takes—especially at times of special stress or pressure—will win you attention, admiration, and a favorable reputation. It will also fortify your backbone.

Acts of God and Why You Need Them

Sometimes, no matter how careful, conscientious, and professional you are, mistakes happen. As a result, you may be blamed for something that was unavoidable. And the rate of such error seems to be increasing as we expand our use of technology.

Here's an example. A designer working at a renowned ad agency was responsible for the creation and production of large outdoor graphic panels. His work and the work of his colleagues were done using computers and electronic file transfers between his agency and the production company.

The production company received his art files electronically, from which proofs were generated for the designer to inspect and approve before production began on the panels. The proofs were smaller in scale than the finished product, but they were quality tested to exacting tolerances. The designer, a man of excellent reputation who took great pride in his work, scrutinized the proofs for accuracy, checking the translation from the smaller-scale proofs to actual-size finished pieces throughout. Satisfied that all was in order, he signed his approval, and production began.

> **The more we love our friends, the less we flatter them; it is by excusing nothing that pure love shows itself.**
>
> MOLIÈRE

When the panels were delivered, there was a three-quarter-inch gap where they should have met, making the pieces unusable. The designer was mortified. The cost to his company to rerun the job was $10,000. He chastised himself severely and hung his head in shame for several days afterward.

As he told me the story, it was obvious that he was deeply troubled and confused by the situation. He was worried about other similar projects in the future and asked how he or anyone else could be expected to prevent such mistakes. He was grateful that his boss had been understanding and compassionate and had not blamed him for the error. Still, he was shaken by what he considered an enormous mistake and a black mark against his professionalism.

An event like this might be considered an "act of God." Sometimes there is no way of preventing errors. Our information, experience, or insights are too limited; the tools or materials are too new; the application too inventive. In situations like these, your best response is to determine what went wrong and to document it. This will help to prevent similar mistakes, although there is no guarantee.

The designer demonstrated admirable backbone in his reaction to the bad news. He listened to understand the problem, acknowledged his participation and final sign-off on the project, and accepted responsibility to resolve the situation. He did not whine about a technology tool he didn't like. He did not try to blame the production company for mishandling the files or ruining his creative work. He did not look around the agency for a scapegoat. These are measures to which people without backbone resort.

An act of God serves as a heads-up, a reminder that things can and do go wrong and that we need to be ever vigilant. It also serves to remind us that sometimes, no matter how closely we attend to things, mistakes will happen anyway. We need to accept this fact and maintain our composure and self-confidence as we seek a workable solution.

There will be other times when we are unjustly berated for mistakes we did not make. As Thomas Paine once said, "These are the times that try men's souls." A word of advice: Hold your tongue. Don't try to explain or justify or to deflect whatever rage is being directed at you. Wait until the storm passes. Take time to think about whether it requires or deserves a rational response. If it does, make notes about the situation as you understand it. Jot down whatever facts you know, including people involved and the time sequence of events. Verify as much of this information as you can before you go back to your critic, and if possible, have a potential solution in hand as well. Discuss the situation calmly, and offer whatever assistance you can provide. Don't point out how you were unjustly attacked. Don't lay blame at someone else's feet. Stick to solving the problem. When you're finished, let it go.

Many people cannot resist responding to an unjustified censure, and their protest is usually delivered at high pitch and high volume. This behavior mirrors that of the attacker and most often results in an escalated situation. More often than not in these cases, the problem remains unsolved, and the emotional debris caused by the heated exchange lingers long afterward. It introduces a level of tension, distrust, and animosity that sours other situations and makes solving future problems more difficult. When you can stop yourself from reacting to attacks, justified or otherwise, you will have taken a giant step toward developing real backbone.

This backbone development will help you avoid the trap of making sorry excuses. It will save you from committing suicide by whining. It will protect you from stabs of betrayal. It will help you gracefully withstand acts of God. The development of a strong backbone will mark you as a person of substance and pride, one worthy of added responsibility, recognition, and reward.

BACKBONE-BUILDING EXERCISES

• *For Competence*
Pay attention to what's going on around you. Listen to the litany of excuses, and note who spouts them.

Where projects routinely jump track, see if glib excuses mask correctible mistakes.

Become aware of your own excuse-making and the situations that tempt you to whine.

• *For Confidence*
Stop yourself in mid-whine. Instead of lobbing a tired excuse, figure out how to rectify an undesirable situation.

At the end of each day, assess the level of responsibility that you assumed for work entrusted to you. Track your progress.

Stay away from people who are habitual excuse makers. Hang around instead with people who find ways to get the job done.

- ***For Risk Taking***

Ask a grumbler to stop complaining and help you work on finding a solution.

Walk away from people who make excuses for not succeeding. By refusing to endorse their behavior, you'll heighten your own awareness of how irresponsible it is and strengthen your resolve to avoid the habit.

Challenge an excuse that's made to you. Say you won't accept it as an answer and that you'll wait for a more responsible reply.

10

Decide What You Think and Say So

WISH I MAY, wish I might, grow a backbone overnight.

Oh, if only it were that easy. But you know it isn't because if it were, you'd have done it by now. Your tentative colleagues would have, too.

The ultimate goal of growing a backbone is to gain the ability to express yourself with confidence and authenticity. To become sure enough of your thoughts and ideas that when others say you're nuts, you're not bothered. To be able to speak up when you need to and hold your ground when assailed. And to be strong enough to wrestle with challenge, happily.

We've talked about the elements of backbone—competence, confidence, and risk taking—and

> **Life shrinks or expands in proportion to one's courage.**
>
> ANAÏS NIN

about strategies for growing one. You're looking now at the ultimate test of backbone: deciding what you think and saying so.

Stop for a second and let that soak in. It's a two-part strategy. First, you're going to decide what you think. Then you're going to share it.

Deciding is active. An important part of exercising your backbone is being an active and purposeful thinker. With a backbone, you don't wonder what you think. You don't let how you feel from moment to moment determine what you think. You don't ask other people to tell you what you think. (There are plenty who will, anyway.) You don't read the paper to see what you think. You decide what you think.

Then you share it. That's active, too. You speak or write or somehow demonstrate what you think.

This process involves many of the strategies we've already talked about. You check out the big picture to develop a context for a particular thought, draw on information from a variety of sources, watch, listen, and think.

For example, when you plan an outdoor activity, you consider the time of year, time of day, and length of event to determine the feasibility of your location. It's basic stuff, I know, but you use this information to decide what you think about holding something outside. It's context stuff. You wouldn't plan an outdoor company meeting in Idaho on January 10. Or in Phoenix on August 5.

Karen and Debbie are in charge of arranging their annual company meeting. They work for a Chicago brokerage firm, and the president wants them to consider holding it outside. They're supposed to give it some thought and get back to him with a recommendation.

Simple enough. An outdoor event in Chicago means a late spring, summer, or early fall date. Temperatures beyond that seasonal window won't work. Even so, spring could be rainy and cold or breezy and mild. Summer could be sunny and dry or overcast and humid; either way, a summer day was likely to be warm and maybe even hot. Fall could be clear and cool or windy and rainy. There's no guarantee on the weather, regardless of the season they pick.

How do they know what the conditions might be? Through experience and, if need be, through the Weather Channel. That's big-picture stuff. It, along with other top-line considerations (number of people and space available, quality of outdoor sound system, presentation logistics), will color the recommendation.

Karen and Debbie privately disagree on a venue. Karen loves outdoor events; Debbie hates them. The first backbone requirement for both women is to be straight about this with each other.

But they're not. So they mind-wrestle for two weeks until Karen finally voices her preference. Outdoors. Then Debbie points out all the technical difficulties that could ruin the event. Karen acknowledges them but reasons that when people are outside, they tend to be more forgiving of that kind of thing. Food is an issue. What people will wear is an issue. What the president has in mind is an issue. Does *he* want the meeting outside? Karen and Debbie wring their hands and debate. They have a very hard time deciding what they think individually; how will they ever come up with a recommendation?

Have you been here? Haven't we all? This is a simple story, but it shows how difficult it can be to decide what you think. Like saying straight-out what movie you want to see. Or what you want for dinner. Or what time you want to meet on Tuesday morning for coffee and which restaurant you prefer.

The need for backbone shows up every time you need to decide something for yourself—hundreds of times each day! And the energy it takes to wrestle with yourself can sap your ambition. Growing a backbone will help you conserve tons of energy for actually doing productive work.

Let's practice. Should you call George now or later? Well, now would be good because . . . why? Because George is a morning person, that's why. He usually completes jobs he starts at the beginning of the day, so you'll have an answer to your question before you go home. Good. Call him now.

Well, later would be good, too, because . . . why? Because you're not entirely sure right now what, specifically, you want to ask for. Or how you should position your request. Nope. You need more time. Call him later.

But if you call him later, you might miss him, and then you wouldn't have your answer by day's end.

But is that important? Maybe a more specific question is better than a quick reply.

Good heavens! Pick one! Decide what you think!

If you call George now with an unframed request, he might, through his own questions, help you clarify what you're after. If, on the other hand, you call him later, you may get his answering service, but you'll be able to leave a concise, precise request. Which is more important to you? Decide what you think, and go for it.

We get into weak-backbone habits because we don't understand how important little things are in determining how we handle big things. If you can't decide when to call someone, how in heaven's name will you decide whether to vote for an acquisition or not? Hire one person over another? Choose a software program from a bunch of look-alike alternatives?

If you can't decide what you think, you'll be at the mercy of others who can. That's why people with backbone run things and people without complain.

But this deciding business isn't quick, easy, or once-and-for-all. It takes time and effort, and it's going to foster anxiety. As you get used to it, the anxiety will ease up, but you're still going to have to put in the time and effort.

Deciding what you think requires that you *do* think. Critically. We've talked about thinking a lot in this book and about ways to see what you think. Note taking, picture drawing, mind mapping—these all show you what's been going on upstairs, and they're great assistants in your decision-making process. If you haven't a clue about what's happening up there (or why), you're going to continue wobbling your way through life.

Critical thinking enables you to consider a situation in all its complexity, identify and appreciate its interrelated elements, understand a ton of implications related to the situation, and reach a decision.

In our crazy, jazzed-up world, there's always something calling to you for attention. There's always more to learn about, think about, and respond to than you can manage. That's why deciding what you think is a backbone essential.

There's a popular notion that able, experienced businesspeople don't need much time to think. That's bunk. The most successful business-people are constant thinkers. They pay attention to life around them, connecting people, places, past events, and bits of seemingly unrelated information to create composites of their current situations.

Thinking requires discipline. It's hard to keep quiet to think when someone is pressuring you for an answer. Successful quick thinkers and decisive executives have paid the dues of time, experience, practice, and learning from past mistakes. Think: Where have you seen something like this before? What did you do? Were you successful? Who else was involved? How did they respond? What would you do differently now if you had the chance? What other choices do you have now? How quickly must you respond? *What do you think?*

Your job demands that you decide what you think about a million propositions a day. These demands are called challenges by the optimistic, problems by less hopeful others. People with backbone see them simply as requirements of the job, and they train themselves to think actively about them. Then they make decisions.

Deciding is the act of firmly choosing one step over another. It takes backbone because any choice can be risky. People with backbone perceive the power of conviction and use it to create a sense of urgency to achieve. They don't waste time in hand-wringing or second-guessing.

People with backbone recognize that others may have feelings and make decisions that differ from theirs. That's OK. They've done their homework and made the best choice given their position and responsibilities. People with backbone don't apologize for their judgments. And they don't reverse themselves when strong opposition drops by.

Saying what you think is impossible without first deciding what you think. I know, duh. That's so obvious that it sounds stupid. But listen to all the people who prattle on, desperately trying to make sense of their thoughts. It's painful. People with backbone know that clear and unambiguous messages result when you decide first and say so second. They speak or write about a decision only after they're satisfied that they've carefully reviewed a situation and reached a firm conclusion.

So, back to those job demands you face. Those challenges. What is your challenge today?

Is today the day you'll decide about making a career move? Will you be straight with your employees about the company's restructuring plans? Will you give honest feedback to a pain-in-the-neck worker?

Will you tell your best manager that he's irresponsible and unproductive when he lets his ego get the best of him? Will you mandate that he pay more attention to what needs doing than what credit is up for grabs? Will you start looking today for better managers?

Will you admit to your senior managers that you're befuddled by recent changes in your industry and that you need their help in figuring out what to do next?

> **He who, when called upon to speak a disagreeable truth, tells it boldly and has done is both bolder and milder than he who nibbles in a low voice and never ceases nibbling.**
>
> JOHANN KASPAR LAVATER (1741–1801)

Will you advise the board of directors that actions you took six months ago have yielded negative results and that your strategy needs to change again?

Will you face reality today?

People with healthy backbones face more realities than weak people do. They share their decisions with others. As they accept and navigate their way through imposing challenges, their competence in doing so grows each time. So does their confidence to face the one ahead. They become willing to risk tense meetings and tough conversations. People with backbone help companies grow, and they're worth every penny they're paid.

Putting It All Together

Jan is the supervisor of a twenty-person accounting department. She is tired of getting dumped on by ill-mannered workers and customers alike, and she's struggling to decide whether or not she should find a different job. Jan knows that the company values her steadfastness and reliability, and she's paid well. But time and time again, people come to her with stupid situations that have spun out of control because someone lied, covered up, lost an invoice, couldn't get an answer to a question, or otherwise didn't do what he or she was supposed to do.

She's tired of errors made within her department. She's had it with her wimpy boss who passes every confrontation on to her. She has zero tolerance left for lazy and irresponsible managers who blame other people for stuff they messed up. She's just plain fed up with everyone's expectation that she act like an adult when nobody else seems compelled to be one.

Jan's discontent has been growing for more than a year, and she's made a couple of halfhearted attempts to find other work. She has a young family at home and, truth be told, feels guilty about the long hours she puts in. And her commute adds an hour each day to her time away from the kids. She's frustrated and, honestly, feels out of control of so many aspects of her life at the moment. Would a new job change things for the better? She realizes with a sigh of resignation that the answer to that question is no. In a new job, she'd have to learn the people, the work, and the quirks of a new organization. Right now, she doesn't have the energy for that. She decides she can put up with her lot for a while yet, until something better comes along.

But how long is a while? And what's the limit of her capacity? Jan hasn't really decided anything other than that she's now tired of thinking about how tired she is. Jan needs to grow a backbone.

Complicated and sensitive pressures impose on our deepest challenges as human beings at work. We hesitate to think much about these ambiguities because the pace of life is so darn swift. Bill Clover, Ph.D., head of the Executive M.B.A. program at Washington University's Olin School of Business, says that one of the greatest challenges for today's executives is managing the dilemma of action versus time to reflect. We worry that if we take the time to step back and consider why we do what we do, what our responsibilities are, and why we continue to go with the flow instead of standing in our own space, we'll never get anything done.

But taking time is precisely what people of backbone do. They force themselves to reflect until it becomes routine. They decide what they think and what they should do about it. They approach each day with clear purpose. They know what they want to accomplish when they make a phone call, send an E-mail message, or write a report. They think about what to expect from others, and they decide how they'll manage these reactions. People with backbone know what they're doing and why.

How good are you at what you do? How intent are you on getting even better? What resources are available to you? How well do you use them? People with backbone make realistic assessments of their professional qualifications. Where they're not happy with the answers, they get busy improving.

As you think about the challenges of your work, where do you look for advice or inspiration? Do you draw from a broad spectrum of resources? Do you feel you have access to help when you need it? Are you comfortable asking for assistance?

What agents influence the pace and direction of your work? Do you control these forces? Some of them? Most of them? None of them?

What obstacles do you typically encounter? How do you overcome them? What do you learn in the process?

If you can develop the habit of asking these questions, thinking deeply about their answers, and realistically determining what the answers mean to you and your career, you'll find inner strengths that will shape a substantial backbone.

Your Time in the Sun

With a strong and reliable backbone, your ability to frame what you think and to say so begins to change how you approach your work. You'll look for opportunities to contribute your perspective and to make decisions that are right for you in specific situations. When you can lay out what you think in unambiguous terms, say plainly why you want to do something, and then take action in the direction you choose, you'll find the clouds of confusion scattering. The rays of power and influence will shine through.

Am I saying you'll be on Easy Street? Not a chance. But you'll be on Confidence Boulevard, and your steps will be a lot firmer than they've been in the past.

Listen to Richard, a marketing vice president, on carrying out a difficult termination:

> I've had the unpleasant task of terminating employees on several occasions throughout my career, but one stands out because it called for a heap of what you call backbone.
>
> The guy I terminated had been recruited to the company a little over a year before I let him go. The person who hired him was no longer with the company, and although there was some connection between them earlier in their careers—which is why he made the move in the first place—that connection was apparently gone.
>
> The guy was bright. Talented, high energy, with a ton of imagination and a great sense of humor. He relocated from another state to take the job, but he'd left his wife and kids at home until he could settle into both the job and the community. His plan was to move the family sometime later. After a year, that plan still hadn't been carried out, so, fortunately, the family hadn't been uprooted.
>
> I met the guy shortly after he came to the company, and although we didn't work together directly, we struck up a friendship. We talked a lot about the company and what we did there. He told hilarious stories about his work with salespeople and clients, and he always had big ideas for new ventures.
>
> I heard from other people that most of his coworkers thought he was nuts. They appreciated his sense of humor and his energy, but geez, his ideas were so out there, they worried about the guy. They were also aware that his knowledge of the industries we served was pretty limited. The general consensus was that for all his great notions, few hit the mark, and some were embarrassingly off base.
>
> As I got to know the guy—his background, skills, and aspirations—I'd come to sincerely appreciate his positive energy and terrific sense of humor. I liked him! But I also thought privately that he was in the wrong place. It seemed obvious to me that he knew next to nothing about the company's busi-

ness and was only vaguely interested in learning about it. I heard a lot of grumbling about how confusing his presentations were to clients and how frustrated and angry internal people were in trying to work with him. I suspected that he wouldn't be around long, and I felt a little sorry for him.

Then he became my problem. Changes in the company opened up his boss's job, and I was lucky enough to get it. You can imagine how hard it was to be this guy's friend one day and his boss the next, especially after all the stuff we'd talked about. What made it worse was that he thought he should have got the job. He was a few years older than I and felt he had more relevant leadership experience. Though he resented being "passed over," as he called it, we were able to have some good talks about the situation. I was relieved about that. I was gratified, too, when he said that although he was disappointed, he respected me and would fully support me in my new role.

But I had a problem. I knew both sides of the story regarding his work— the good side from him, the not-so-good side from his colleagues. And while I didn't want to confront him based on hearsay—even his own—I knew I had to address his spotty performance. I didn't think that rehashing the past would be of much use, so I decided instead to review his current progress on his projects.

Over the next couple of weeks, we met often to talk about his projects. During that same period, I got a bunch of unpleasant phone calls from salespeople and his coworkers. They wanted me to "do something about him."

As I thought about the whole situation, I realized I had to move the guy out. The alienation of both clients and internal staff was dangerous—to me as well as to the company—and I didn't see any good way to change that. I did want, if possible, to help him find something more suitable to his abilities because I respected his energy and ideas. I thought a long time about what to do, and I was convinced that termination was the right conclusion. I went to the head of human resources to tell her this and to get her advice on how best to handle it. I was surprised to run into a buzz saw.

"You can't terminate him! We'll have an age discrimination suit on our hands!"

I hadn't thought about that. The guy was in his late forties.

Then she started to lecture me. "You can't terminate him just because you think he's in the wrong place. You have to show cause. You have to document how he's screwing things up and how it's hurting the company. You have to have evidence."

This didn't sit well with me, and I tried to explain all the discussions I'd had with the guy and the stories I'd heard from salespeople and clients. I admitted they were anecdotal, but I said I thought they showed strong enough reason to make this decision.

But HR was dead against doing anything fast. She got our corporate attorney on the line, and we had a three-hour conference call about all the possible litigation that could result from a hasty termination. Stating my case as frankly and completely as I could, I said I felt strongly that any significant delay would create greater cause for concern. I told them I believed my best strategy was to be straight with the guy. I said that I'd got to know him pretty well and that although he'd be surprised, hurt, and probably embarrassed as hell, I was convinced that he'd respect the honesty. I went so far as to say he'd probably agree with my assessment and in all likelihood would be relieved to be set free in a dignified and compassionate way.

But again, HR and the corporate attorney didn't buy it, and they warned me pretty sternly not to do anything immediate. They insisted I make book on the guy for thirty days, write him up several times in the course of the month, and confront him with this evidence to justify his termination. Of course, this was all said with the utmost political correctness, but the message was clear.

In my mind, it was a terrible strategy. First of all, the guy was not bad or deficient in the main; he simply didn't fit our environment. Second, I was extremely disappointed to be advised to take a roundabout approach to what seemed to me a fairly straightforward problem. Argue as I would, the HR pros didn't budge. They said there are safe methods for dealing with terminations, and any challenge to the methods carried substantial risk.

I batted around the problem all that night. I made lists of pros and cons. I wrote out all the scenarios I could think of regarding possible lawsuits and why the guy would or would not be prone to act on them. I replayed our conversations of the past year and applied everything I'd learned about him. I envisioned the dialogue we'd have if I fired him and tried to anticipate his reactions. I became more convinced that honesty and directness were the best methods to use in confronting the man. Anything short of these would betray the respect I knew he had for me as a person, though I tried in every way I could to recast the situation as "purely business." By morning, I had decided to go ahead with the termination, in direct disobedience to the advice given me by HR and our attorney.

(Did you hear that? He decided what he thought.)

When I got to the office, I poured a cup of coffee, checked my calendar to make sure I had no early appointments, then stood in my doorway and took a deep breath. I knew the man would be in his office—he was always there at least forty-five minutes early—and I wanted to "do the deed" before others got there.

As I walked toward his office, I had huge second thoughts. I worried, I wondered, and I almost turned back. But I'd thought very carefully about the situation, and I knew that what I was about to do was the right thing for him as well as for the company.

We spent a few minutes exchanging morning greetings, and then I dived right in.

I told him I'd been struggling with a difficult problem that concerned him and I wanted to talk about it. I told him that I appreciated his incredible energy and sense of humor and that I liked some of his ideas for the areas of business he was most knowledgeable about and interested in. Then I explained the company's major clients and the kinds of work we did most successfully for them. He was quick to pick up the mismatch.

I told him how the mismatch created confusion and frustration for our salespeople and his coworkers. I told him that the quality of his work suffered when he couldn't get the cooperation he needed and that his reputation was taking a hit because of it. After a few minutes of laying out my thoughts, I simply said he was a bright and talented guy who was in the wrong place. I said that I'd work with him on a separation timetable but that he had two weeks tops to clean out his office. I also said I wanted his company credit cards—he had two of them—but that he could keep his entrance key until he was finished moving his things out.

To say the guy was surprised is an understatement. He was shocked. Hurt. He couldn't believe what I was telling him. For twenty minutes, he paced around his office, swearing and shouting. He even threw a folder or two. He told me all the reasons why he should have been promoted to my job. He told me where the company was missing the boat on opportunities. He said that he didn't know why he had hung around such a loser place for so long anyway and that he'd be glad to finally get the hell out.

I sat in silence. I respected his frustration, and truthfully, I thought he made some good points. I thought the venting was helpful. At least, I hoped it was. Eventually, we'd have to talk about how to make our parting of ways as graceful as possible for him and for the company, and I wanted him to be a little calmer when we did that.

All told, we spent an hour and a half that morning talking things over. When we finished, he left the building. I told him that I wouldn't say anything to the rest of the group until the following day and that if he wanted to talk some more, he should call me.

Did I overdo it spending so much time with him? Maybe. I knew it was absolutely against standard protocol. But I respected the man, and I felt it was important to demonstrate this. I wanted to spare him whatever indignity I could. But I have to admit I was also keenly aware of the potential for a law-suit. I wanted to give him no reason, however small, to think seriously about suing us. I counted on the fact that he'd remember some of the wild things he'd said during our meeting and decide that litigation would be foolish.

The story has an OK ending. The guy left the company within the week. He brought cookies for our group on his last day. There were lots of hugs and funny stories as we stood in the entryway saying good-bye. I never heard another word from him after that day. I assume he moved back to his home state, but I never heard. There were no lawsuits filed, either.

How did I deal with HR? I called to confess my transgression and recount the story of the termination. She wasn't there, so I left a voice-mail message. Then I called the company president to tell him what I'd done, but he was out for the day.

When the president and I met a day or two later, I got a tongue-lashing for my foolishness, and I was warned never to do such a stupid thing again. I took my medicine in silence. I was fully aware of the embarrassment and frustration the human resources manager felt, and I was sympathetic. On the other hand, I was convinced that I'd done the right thing. I'm happy and prob-ably lucky to say that the incident didn't create any lingering ill will for any of us. We respected each other's positions, and although we had serious dif-ferences, the end result was that the job got done effectively.

This is backbone at its finest. He decided what he thought after long and careful consideration, and then he said so. Acted on it, too, which is the all-important risk-taking aspect of exercising a healthy backbone.

What would you do in a tough situation? Are you ready to test your backbone? Are you prepared to pay attention to what's on your mind and make some decisions about it? Would you then be able to act on them? Let's see.

You and Bob are working together to develop a new product, and you gather with a research and development pro to discuss progress. The

R&D guy presents results of a test he conducted on the material you plan to use for the product. His research shows that at certain temperatures the material becomes unstable—it warps at high temperatures and tends to crack in cold temperatures. You make note of this. As the discussion continues, you notice that Bob is shaking his head and resisting the information. He wants to use the material because it has special characteristics that he has not found in other materials. He believes its uniqueness makes it especially effective for the project. Furthermore, he has already shown it to potential customers and has convinced them that this new product is going to be hot. They, in turn, are eager to be the first to own the new product.

You wonder how your customers will react when their new product proves defective as temperatures change. You worry about shipping it during hot and cold seasons. You worry about customers' storage climates and how the product will tolerate changes. You wonder what tolerances the product has for jostling and handling under any climatic circumstances.

You ask these questions matter-of-factly, hoping that Bob will pay attention and realize that his preference for this material is fraught with danger. You note the researcher's responses, growing more concerned as the meeting goes on. Your focus is on the customer while Bob's and the R&D guy's are on their own perspectives and stubbornly held positions. Bob's not making notes—he didn't bring a pad of paper to the meeting. Neither did the R&D guy. He has copies of his report and scratched a few notes on the back of one of the pages, but beyond that, there's little being recorded about this discussion.

After the meeting, you follow Bob to his office and ask for his thoughts. Bob says the R&D guy is lobbying as he always does. "Dr. No is determined to shut down another one of my projects, and this time I'm not going to let him." You let this pass.

Reading from your notes, you ask again about the vulnerability of the material to changes in temperature. Bob says the dangers are overstated, that within the ranges typical for most customers, there is no problem. You ask how Bob can be sure of this. He says, simply, "I've been around here long enough. I just know." Besides, he admits to you, he has already negotiated a great price on the material, which will allow the company to make a healthy margin on the product even with modest sales volumes.

Your dilemma now as a member of the project team is whether to pursue the potential trouble spots that make you uncomfortable or let Bob run with the project. You know Bob. You know he's convinced of his position, and you respect his experience and grit in holding his ground. You find the prospects of a healthy margin attractive. You're not as familiar with the R&D guy. You don't know where he's coming from. Could he be spinning data to flaunt Bob? Is he making a big deal out of something negligible?

You review your notes again, ruminate about all the project information you have to date, and try to decide if you should make one more attempt to bring the two sides of the debate to some consensus. The question ultimately is: Should you stick your neck out or hide behind Bob's certainty?

What will you do?

If your backbone is weak or nonexistent, you'll play your uncertainties to the hilt. You'll worry about how your friendship with Bob will be damaged if you push your position. You'll wonder if the R&D guy has more clout (because if he does, you might push it). You'll get depressed about why *you* should have to be the one contending with this when Bob's the one causing the problem. Well, no, maybe it's the R&D guy who's creating static. Oh, just forget it. It's way too complicated, and there's no way you can win if you press it. Besides, it's Bob's problem, not yours.

If, on the other hand, you have a backbone, you realize that comfortable or not, sticking your neck out is the right posture in this instance. You prepare a brief outline of particulars to discuss and gather the group once again. Your notes and careful consideration give you stature in the meeting. Because you've documented, objectively, what the salient points are, you have some influence over the discussion. The outcome may not satisfy you entirely, but by taking responsibility for resolving disparate opinions, you exercise your backbone to act on what you think.

What happens when you decide what you think and then say so? People pay attention! And when you do what you say you're going to do based on what you think, you'll be walking the talk—a most impressive (and unusual) backbone activity. This, by the way, builds a strong foundation for trust. It becomes a self-fulfilling kind of thing. When you think with backbone, decide with backbone, and act with backbone, you'll have a backbone on which not only you, but also others, depend.

The net result is that you feel stronger and more confident, which makes people see you in a new light and brings expanded opportunity and influence. While your backbone won't let you bask in the sun for long (there's always something to be done), it will warm you with feelings of self-assurance and success.

Measuring Your Magic

So, how will you measure your growing backbone? What reliable tools can you use to be sure you're making progress? Maybe a densitometer? You know, that gadget medics use to gauge the thickness of your bones. Don't think so.

How about a wall chart, so you can follow how much taller you are as your backbone solidifies? Not a bad idea, but that'd be too easy to manipulate.

Maybe a written test of some sort that can show your progression through higher scores? That might be comforting, but nope.

The best and surest way to measure your backbone magic is to measure your new demeanor. Pay attention to the things you do now that you didn't do before. Monitor the number and quality of interactions you have now with other people that you didn't before. Keep score of how many times you offer your opinions, ideas, or suggestions. The stronger you get, the more comfortable you'll be in sharing what you think.

As your backbone develops, you'll decide more surely what you think, and you'll be more willing to say so. This doesn't necessarily mean you'll be more outspoken or participative on a daily basis, because as your backbone grows, you'll also learn to pick your battles more astutely. But you'll feel more certain about how you got to your opinions, and you'll understand just what you intend to accomplish when you share them.

Keep track of how many people defer to your opinion. Watch how many turn to you in meetings in anticipation of your thoughts. See how much more often your phone rings as people call to touch base with you. Monitor the number and types of new assignments you get. Track your promotions.

Perhaps the most wonderful way of measuring a strong and healthy backbone is to gauge your increasing willingness to take responsibility for yourself. To take a level-headed approach to your business challenges, to admit mistakes, review situations objectively, accept criticism with grace and an attitude of learning, and recognize that the goal is not perfection, but rather continual progress toward improvement.

When you grow a backbone, you'll own your thoughts and decisions. You'll no longer blame superiors, friends, the weather, society, or your health for difficulties, disappointments, or setbacks. You'll continue to work toward your goals with purpose and hope. You'll mitigate the fall-out from unexpected events and reactions to your efforts, and you'll think about what they mean. You'll find other ways to approach and resolve problems, aware that you'll always have choices. Most of all, when you find yourself in stressful, high-stakes situations, you'll celebrate your backbone when instead of feeling weak in the knees and sick to your stomach, you feel taller, lighter, and much, much stronger. (And when those nasty days barge in—they will, you know—you'll be able to take them in stride, knowing that they're a natural part of life, not some kind of cosmic proof that you're deficient.)

To conclude, I'd like to share my own story of backbone glory and challenge you to get busy on one of your own.

I was the newest leader of a failing marketing division, and it was time to announce a new order. We were set for a divisionwide meeting to unveil a new team structure, announce team leaders, and set guidelines regarding business processes. The event was scheduled for Monday at 3:00 P.M. at a hotel near our headquarters. On the Friday before the meeting, I got a call from the senior VP and general manager of the company's other operating division. It was 4:00 P.M., and he was calling me from his car on his way home for the weekend. He told me I could not hold my meeting the following Monday. Surprised and puzzled by this call at the eleventh hour, I asked him why. He said simply, "Because you're not ready."

"What do you mean I'm not ready? I don't understand."

"I don't think you know what you're doing. I don't think you'll be able to answer questions."

Though I was incensed at this flippant challenge from someone who had paid no attention to the work we'd done over the past six months, I patiently explained some of it. "We've met in small groups and large groups. We've tracked our business and analyzed where we're making money and where we're not. We've assessed everyone in the division to match talent and experience with client needs. We've met numerous times with HR to revise all position descriptions and to assign pay ranges based on the point system used throughout the rest of the company. We are ready."

"No, I still think you're going to have questions you can't answer."

Frustrated and angry but inspired by an idea, I managed to keep my voice calm and my manner light. "OK," I said, "here's what we'll do. You spend this weekend jotting down as many questions as you can think of. On Monday morning, we'll play Stump the Chump. If I can't answer even one of your questions, I'll call off the meeting."

Still maintaining that I didn't know what I was doing, my challenger reluctantly agreed and hung up.

On Monday morning, my phone was silent. No call from my challenger. No list of questions. No follow-through on his objection.

I went ahead with the meeting. I was fully prepared, well organized, and able to answer all questions that arose. At a reception following the meeting, my challenger approached me with a sheepish look. "Nice job," was all he said.

My main message in telling this story is that sometimes you have to stand your ground, regardless of where a challenge originates. This person, though my counterpart in a different division, had a greater measure of power and influence than I did. He was a shareholder of the firm; I was not. He had nearly twenty years' experience in the organization; I had seven. His division represented the core competence of the company, along with the history and tradition of success the company had enjoyed for more than fifty years. My division was an adolescent by comparison and an unprofitable one for the past several years. My assignment at the time was to restore its profitability.

> **The future of mankind lies waiting for those who will come to understand their lives and take up their responsibilities to all living things.**
>
> VINE VICTOR DELORIA JR.

I could have been intimidated out of my meeting. I did give second and serious thought to the magnitude of what I was about to do. I spent the weekend before the meeting soul-searching. Had we done everything we needed to do? Had we asked the right questions? Had we dug deep enough for answers? Were we being responsible in making these changes? What were the implications of launching this new structure within the traditional organization? Would I be able to support these people as they began working in new ways? Had I overstepped my own capabilities and the collective capabilities of the people within the division?

As I reviewed the scope and depth of our work, I was comfortable and confident. We had been thorough and conscientious. Early on, we had asked for and received the support of the president. We had worked with the internal groups that we would need to support our efforts. We had communicated clearly and continuously. We knew we would encounter resistance within the organization, and we had discussed ways to counteract it. Although we had no guarantees of success, we were ready to begin something new.

If I had hesitated or backed down in the face of an ill-founded objection, I would have betrayed the hard work and trust of thirty-five people who believed in what we were doing and understood where we were going.

The second point of this story is that people will, from time to time, do and say outrageous things. This man had no business challenging my work in such a cavalier manner. His objections were ill informed and unfounded. The proof of this was borne out in his lack of follow-through. He believed that by flat-out forbidding me to hold my meeting, he could put a stop to the plans we had made for change. When I held my ground, he became confused. I learned later that he was angry, too. He had counted on the power imbalance in which he held more cards to effectively shut me down.

This kind of attempted power move is not uncommon in business. It is especially prevalent where imbalances of power do exist. The best remedy is due diligence, careful thought, attention to detail, and firm decision making.

Still another point I want to emphasize in this story is the manner in which I responded to the challenge. Had I reacted with all the indignation I felt, I would have hurt my own position. The challenge was issued in an undisciplined and unprofessional manner. That it came from a senior officer gave it import and made it a charge I could not brush aside. I had to meet it head-on. But to engage in a shouting match or any battle on his terms would have meant sure defeat for me.

Certainly, I was offended. I had been forbidden to hold a decisive meeting via a car phone call from a guy who was on his way home for the weekend. A guy who, yes, was a player in the company but who had not clue one about anything we had worked on for the past six months. A guy who, in fact, had been sniping at the failing division for months but who had never had the guts to address me or anyone else directly. What audacity!

And the fact that he couldn't give me any better reason for canceling my meeting than "You won't be able to answer questions" was appallingly irresponsible in my mind. This, from a senior officer? Wow.

At any rate, I couldn't afford to let him rattle me. Knowing what was at stake and uncertain of how or whether he would continue to push me, I decided to maintain a friendly, easy manner. This confused him. He had expected me to become upset and defensive and to outline, chapter and verse, the work we had done, hoping to gain his blessing. When I gave him a simple summary and suggested he challenge me with questions, I beat him at his own game. I didn't know, when I suggested this, that he would back down. I was sincere in my offer to cancel the meeting if I were unable to reasonably answer his questions. By inviting him to challenge me fairly and professionally, I put the responsibility back where it belonged. On him. This, of course, was the last thing he wanted.

Had his concern been genuine, he would have taken time much earlier to understand what we were doing and to appraise our objectives and our solutions. He certainly would not have chosen to shoot from the hip as he had.

As I waited for his call on Monday morning, I had a healthy hunch it wouldn't come. I was tempted at one point to call him and ask how many questions he had. But the ball was in his court, and I didn't necessarily want it back in mine. I privately hoped that he was embarrassed by his show of unprofessionalism and lack of support, but I suspected he had given it little thought since hanging up his car phone several days before.

My Stump the Chump challenge stopped him in his tracks. It was a risk, I realized that, but it was a risk worth taking. And it paid dividends.

As you consider whether or not to take a particular risk at work—to exercise your backbone—take time to decide what you think. Reflect as much as you need to. Draw pictures, take notes, go for long walks, have your friends play Jeopardy with your answers, do whatever you need to do to get your head straight about what you're facing. Realize that sometimes your decisions are going to be unpopular and that if they bear on a lot of people, you may be in for more argument than you'd like. That's OK. That's why you're growing a backbone.

This book derives from my conviction that anyone who wants to can take hold of his or her future through the building of a strong backbone. You can't make excuses for why now is not a good time. Just decide that it is and get busy.

Growing a backbone gives you the freedom to claim the authenticity of your person and your life. It's a kick, believe me. Why be a plow horse when you can be a unicorn?

Grow a backbone. Get a life. Your company will exalt in your success. Let that business renaissance begin!

Godspeed.

BACKBONE-BUILDING EXERCISES

• *For Competence*

While your thoughts run, skip, and jump, practice catching them. Ask yourself, What do I think about this? Corral your thoughts into separate pens, then step back to see where you stand.

Practice deciding what you think. Read a newspaper or magazine article. Decide what the main point of the piece is (yes, I know this can be difficult), and ask yourself, "What do I think?" See if you agree or disagree with the author, and practice outlining why.

• *For Confidence*

Trade thoughts with others. After you decide what you think (you like Joe's Restaurant better than Sally's Diner because . . .), share your decision. Watch the reaction. (You may find lots of great restaurants this way!)

Take an opposing stance once in a while to practice your decision-making skills. Say, for example, Lester wants to go to a software training class and is debating the cost. Tell him you think it's a bad investment, and say why. (Don't get too intense here; it's practice!)

- *For Risk Taking*

Introduce a controversial nonwork topic (anything from sports or politics is perfect), and say what you've decided about the subject. Start with something outside of work because controversy gets emotions running high, and you don't want your potentially discordant views to damage your professional standing.

Dare to say "I've decided this" about something. Be prepared to summarize how you got to your conclusion and what you considered along the way.

Walk around to the other side of the table. Take a look at the evidence from that perspective, and see how it influences your thinking. If you decide something different from each side of the table, you've got more thinking to do!

Bibliography

Bartlett, John. *Bartlett's Familiar Quotations, Fifteenth and 125th Anniversary Edition.* Boston: Little, Brown and Company, 1980.

Cooper, Robert K. and Ayman Sawaf. *Executive EQ: Emotional Intelligence in Leadership and Organizations.* New York: Grosset/Putnam, 1997.

Dertouzos, Michael. *What Will Be: How the New World of Information Will Change Our Lives.* New York: HarperCollins Publishers, Inc., 1997.

Drucker, Peter F. *Managing for the Future: The 1990s and Beyond.* New York: Truman Talley Books/Dutton, 1992.

Gardner, John W. *On Leadership.* New York: Free Press, 1989.

George, Stephen. *Uncommon Sense: Creating Business Excellence in Your Organization.* New York: John Wiley & Sons, Inc., 1997.

Goleman, Daniel. *Emotional Intelligence.* New York: Bantam Books, 1995.

———. *Working With Emotional Intelligence.* New York: Bantam Books, 1998.

Hamel, Gary and C. K. Prahalad. *Competing for the Future.* Boston: Harvard Business School Press, 1994.

Handy, Charles. "Noteworthy Quotes." *Strategy & Business* (Fourth Quarter, 1998) 67.

Joiner, Brian L. *Fourth Generation Management.* New York: McGraw-Hill, Inc., 1994.

Jones, Glenn R. "Creating a Leadership Organization with a Learning Mission." *The Organization of the Future.* San Francisco: Jossey-Bass, 1997.

Kao, John. *Jamming.* New York: HarperCollins Publishers, Inc., 1996.

Kotter, John P. *The New Rules: Eight Business Breakthroughs to Career Success in the 21st Century.* New York: Simon & Schuster, Inc., 1995.

————.*Leading Change.* Boston: Harvard Business School Press, 1996.

Kouzes, James M. and Barry Z. Posner. *Credibility.* San Francisco: Jossey-Bass, 1993.

Maltz, Maxwell, M.D., F.I.C.S. *Psycho-Cybernetics.* Englewood Cliffs, NJ: Prentice Hall, Inc., 1960.

Matsushita, Konosuke. "Noteworthy Quotes." *Strategy & Business* (Fourth Quarter, 1998) 67.

Micklethwait, John and Adrian Wooldridge. *The Witch Doctors: Making Sense of the Management Gurus.* New York: Random House, Inc., 1996.

Nadler, David A. and Janet L. Spencer and Associates. *Executive Teams.* San Francisco: Jossey-Bass, 1998.

The New York Public Library Desk Reference. New York: Simon & Schuster, Inc., 1989.

Peter, Dr. Laurence J. *The Peter Principle.* New York: Buccaneer Books, 1996.

Prahalad, C. K. "The Work of New Age Managers in the Emerging Competitive Landscape." *The Organization of the Future.* San Francisco: Jossey-Bass, 1997.

Reichheld, Frederick F. *The Loyalty Effect.* Boston: Bain & Company, Inc., 1996.

Ryan, Kathleen D. and Daniel K. Oestreich. *Driving Fear Out of the Workplace.* San Francisco: Jossey-Bass, 1992.

Schein, Edgar H. *Organizational Culture and Leadership.* Second Edition. San Francisco: Jossey-Bass, 1992.

Senge, Peter. *The Fifth Discipline: The Art & Practice of the Learning Organization.* New York: Doubleday Books, 1990.

Sethi, Deepak. "The Seven Rs of Self-Esteem." *The Organization of the Future.* San Francisco: Jossey-Bass, 1997.

Taylor, Jim and Watts Walker. *The 500 Year Delta: What Happens After What Comes Next.* New York: HarperCollins Publishers, Inc., 1997.

Ulrich, Dave. "Organizing Around Capabilities." *The Organization of the Future.* San Francisco: Jossey-Bass, 1997.

Index